Countryside recreation in a changing society

Carolyn Harrison

DEPARTMENT OF GEOGRAPHY
UNIVERSITY COLLEGE LONDON

Published by
The TMS Partnership Ltd. London
1991

ISBN: 1 872256 26 0

First published in 1991 by The TMS Partnership Ltd.
Text and cover design by Design Locker, Bristol
Cover photograph by Liane Bradbrook
Printed by Booksprint, Bristol

Copies available from the author:

Geography Department
University College London
26 Bedford Way
London WC1H 0AP

Acknowledgements

This book has its origins in two research projects funded by the Economic and Social Research Council with additional financial assistance from the Countryside Commission for England and Wales. I am pleased to acknowledge their support. I would also like to thank colleagues who collaborated with me on these projects and research assistants Martin Ferguson, Sue Walker and Melanie Limb who kept us to the task in hand.

Richard Munton, Philip Lowe and Jacquie Burgess spent time reviewing earlier drafts of the text as did my mother. I am most grateful to them all for their help and encouragement.

Several other people have contributed to the production process. I would like to thank especially Robert Bradbrook in the Cartographic Unit, Department of Geography, University College London, who designed most of the illustrations, and Jane Stevenson and Helen Locker of Design Locker for their advice and professionalism.

My family has lived with 'the book' for some time and I owe them a special debt. So thankyou Kate and Daniel for putting up with me when I retreated to the study and most of all thanks to John for making it happen.

Contents

....

Introduction

In recent debates about the future of the British countryside, less emphasis has been given to the role recreation might play in shaping the appearance and functioning of the countryside than has been devoted to agricultural and forestry interests. One of the purposes of this book is to redress this imbalance in the belief that to underestimate the importance of countryside recreation is to misrepresent what living in modern society means. For, as other commentators have remarked (Urry, 1988, Veal, 1987), the amount of leisure time available to adults and children alike sets modern society apart from its predecessors and what people do in their leisure time has a profound effect upon the way society functions. Importantly too, people have come to place differing values on particular leisure environments and activities especially those associated with the countryside. In this way social and cultural changes merge imperceptibly together and the leisure activities and the environments people enjoy are constantly redefined as society itself changes.

How modern society has come to define its recreational relationship with the countryside forms the central theme of this study. Critically, the book seeks to address the following questions:

* Why is visiting the countryside so popular?

* Why in contemporary debates about the countryside are some outdoor activities and not others regarded as appropriate in the countryside?

* Why have public sector policies for recreation focused on particular sites rather than on the wider countryside most people enjoy?

* How will the new recreational demands made by contemporary society be accommodated in the countryside?

Approach and major themes

The results of various surveys undertaken in the 1980s show that countryside recreation is a truly popular activity. After socializing, visiting the countryside is the most popular activity which takes place outside the home (Veal, 1984) and recent estimates suggest that as many as 18 million trips are made into the countryside on a typical summer Sunday (Countryside Commission, 1985). The General Household Survey (OPCS, 1986) also reveals that 32% of the adult population take part in at least one outdoor activity such as sports, games and physical activities during the year and amongst these activities middle-distance walking (2 miles or more) is the most popular. 19% of all adults had gone for a walk of two miles or more during the four weeks before the interview.

Given the size of this constituency it is not surprising to find that countryside recreation embraces a wide range of outdoor activities and takes place in a wide variety of environmental and social settings (Countryside Commission, 1987a, Centre for Leisure Research, 1986). The definition of countryside recreation adopted here reflects this spectrum of activities and environments. It includes outdoor activities like mountaineering, climbing, walking, canoeing and fishing irrespective of whether these activities are organized or not. It also includes activities like golf and motor sports which take place in a countryside setting because lack of space or anti-social considerations like noise, prevent them from taking place in the urban area. In this way countryside recreation is defined empirically rather than conceptually, geographically or institutionally. It includes for example, hill walking and strolling, white-water canoeing and pleasure boating, blood sports and nature study, horse racing and horse riding. Characteristically too, countryside recreation includes pleasure motoring and stopping off in the countryside to picnic, admire the view, visit a pub or pick-your-own farm (Glyptis, 1991).

This empirical definition serves to emphasise the diverse ways in which the countryside is enjoyed and contrasts with the rather more selective view of countryside recreation often adopted in public debates about recreation. On their own however, the niceties of definitions do not provide adequate explanations for the fact that some outdoor activities find a place in the countryside whilst others do not. Neither do they explain why recreation provision is largely discussed in terms of facilities and sites rather than in terms of a right of citizenship all people can benefit from. By placing countryside recreation in its wider social and cultural setting, this study aims to demonstrate that countryside recreation is a distinctive leisure activity determined both by how society is organized and by how particular powerful groups in society have come to determine what countryside recreation means.

A cultural perspective on countryside recreation

Several studies of modern society (Lowe and Goyder, 1983, Newby, 1988, Elson, 1986, Countryside Commission, 1987) have shown how environmental groups, farmers, local residents, planning authorities, public agencies and some sports organizations, regard only some recreational uses appropriate for the countryside and not others. As a result, proposals for additional recreational facilities in the country-side are often opposed because they represent a form of 'development' which threatens what the countryside itself has come to mean. At the same time, calls for new legislation and an access charter which would secure public rights of access to the countryside have consis-tently foundered throughout the modern period because they were opposed by those private landowning interests which play such a cen-tral role in British society. So, although countryside recreation is taken for granted as part of modern life, the recreational use of the countryside is constrained both by people's knowledge of their rights when out in the countryside and by the attitudes of landowners towards recreation itself.

One of the purposes of this study is to show how differing ideologies of the countryside and its 'proper' enjoyment have played an impor-tant part in shaping what countryside recreation has come to mean. In particular, it seeks to examine how differing ideologies have influenced the relative ease with which people are able to enjoy and gain access to the recreational environments they seek. The study draws on the concept of 'accessibility' as both a social and cultural construct to express the extent to which different groups of recre-ationalists can enjoy the environments and activities they seek – when, how and where they wish (Countryside Commission, 1986). By approaching the study in this way, countryside recreation is seen to have been defined by society in particular ways at different points in time and public sector policies can also be assessed as part of this pro-cess. Viewed from this perspective, countryside recreation in modern society is seen to be a cultural legacy which enshrines many of the atti-tudes and values of society in the past as well as reflecting the contin-uing influence of proprietorial rights.

Chapters 2 and 3 illustrate how many of today's attitudes to country-side recreation have their origin in the nineteenth and early twentieth centuries when a rapidly urbanizing society began to redefine its recreational relationship with the countryside. At this time, state intervention in recreational policies was minimal, although by the 1930s, several county authorities had taken steps to both provide for recreation and influence where and what recreational activities took place in the countryside. Interestingly, this historical perspective reveals that the ways in which most new recreational demands have been accommodated in the countryside since this time, owe much to the persistence of environmental attitudes consolidated before car-based recreation became truly popular and before the state took a more prominent role in countryside recreation policies. Moreover, many of the organizations which sought to ensure that the countryside was accessible for outdoor recreation were established in this period too and the beliefs and activities of these organizations have themselves had a profound effect upon the way countryside recreation is now defined.

The emphasis given to the post-war period in Chapters 4–8 reflects the popularity accorded to countryside recreation since the 1950s and the increasing involvement of the public sector in recreation policy and provision after 1949. Indeed the very popularity of countryside recreation prompted central government to intervene deliberately in people's enjoyment of the countryside through enacting the National Parks Act. This legislation was designed to protect highly valued countryside areas and access to them. By 1950 Forest Parks and National Parks had been established, and in 1968 The Countryside Act transformed the National Parks Commission into the Countryside Commission and extended its remit to the wider countryside.[1] This new remit reflected the mounting concern expressed by many powerful groups in society about the 'threat' countryside recreation posed. Local authority planners and elected members, rural landowners and environmental groups came to regard mass participation in countryside recreation as a threat to the very essence of all that the countryside symbolized and Structure Plans prepared by county authorities at this time came to reflect this mounting concern. Important to the argument developed here is the fact that the 1968 Act, under which

---

1. The 1968 Countryside Act established the Countryside Commission for England and Wales (hereafter referred to as the Countryside Commission). A separate organization, the Countryside Commission for Scotland had been established a year earlier in 1967 under The Countryside (Scotland) Act. In 1991, under the Environment Protection Bill, the Countryside Commission for Wales was merged with the regional office of the Nature Conservancy Council to create the Countryside Council for Wales. A similar merger will take place in Scotland in 1992. The Countryside Commission for England retains its separate identity, based at Cheltenham.

the Countryside Commission was established, did not define the countryside or open air recreation. As a result, how countryside recreation came to be defined, studied and planned in the public arena was influenced profoundly by the attitudes and values underpinning the Commission's interpretation and administration of its remit.

The Commission's dual responsibility for both countryside recreation and countryside conservation meant that recreation was unlikely to be treated on its own merits, but the fact that it became regarded as a threat rather than an opportunity to be grasped, cannot be explained merely by the Commission's dual responsibilities. Wider social changes also had their influence on the Commission's thinking and activities. Chapter 3 shows how the environmental attitudes and sensitivities of several groups and organizations concerned with the countryside were often arrayed together, *against* the interests of outdoor recreation. How the Commission came to represent the interests of informal countryside recreation – and the Sports Council those interests of outdoor pursuits – cannot therefore be divorced from other aspects of society. The rise of modern environmentalism and the dominance of technocentric attitudes among groups in society in a position of power had a particularly pervasive influence as Pepper (1986) has shown. An appraisal of the extent to which the interests of 'unorganized' users of the countryside for informal outdoor recreation were represented in public policies of this period, illustrates these interrelationships well. It suggests, like Pepper before, that cultural filters – attitudes and values – serve to influence the way in which countryside recreation became identified as a problem to be managed rather than an opportunity to provide a genuine improvement in people's lives. In this way a culture of public intervention served to contain where and how people enjoyed themselves *and* masqueraded as a social policy which would benefit everyone.

Further justification for this proposition is provided by a detailed examination of the attitudes and values held by people who seek to visit the countryside for recreational purposes and the views of providers and landowners who control access to it. Chapter 4 illustrates that the diversity of views expressed by the public contrasts strongly with the unanimity expressed by providers and landowners about appropriate recreational use and the inviolability of property rights for determining access to the countryside. It suggests that the plurality of values held by the participating public are not reflected in the policies adopted in the public arena especially when those policies are designed to act in the interests of informal countryside recreation. Together these chapters suggest that the general direction taken by public policies has not served the interests of informal recreation very effectively neither has it raised participation levels amongst people who have no recent tradition of visiting the countryside. Rather, it has served to ensure that the balance of interest continues to lie with private landowners.

A social perspective on countryside recreation

During the the 1970s social policies designed to raise participation levels in outdoor sport and countryside recreation were pursued by both the Sports Council and the Countryside Commission. 'Sport for All' and 'Recreation for All' became slogans which epitomized the social dimension of these policies. The Sports Council with its stronger promotional remit pursued this policy most consistently (McIntosh and Charlton, 1985) but, social considerations also played a part in the policies pursued by the Countryside Commission (Coalter et al. 1986).

Much of the early impetus for these policies came from a realization that structural changes in post-war western economies and in the work patterns and leisure time of most people would generate new recreational demands. More people enjoyed long holidays with pay and a short working week, and estimates made in the early 1970s suggested that by the end of the 1980s full-time manual workers in the manufacturing industries could have leisure time half as long as their working time. One of the concerns central government expressed was that people would use this new found leisure time constructively rather than irresponsibly (McIntosh and Charlton, 1985); concerns which echoed those of the rational recreation movement of the nineteenth century. A second concern related to the fact that while several studies had shown outdoor recreation to be a popular activity, some people participated regularly and some not at all. Non-participants were found most often amongst lower socio-economic groups, young people and the elderly. This realization together with the spectre of forced unemployment amongst workers in traditional heavy industries and early retirement amongst an already ageing population, led a Labour Government favourably disposed to social welfare objectives to develop policies designed to promote outdoor recreation for everyone.

The range of initiatives taken as part of these socially-motivated policies fell into two broad categories – those directed to particular target areas (the inner city and the urban fringe) and those directed to particular target groups (the 'disadvantaged', and particular user-groups). The effectiveness of these two approaches in raising participation levels in outdoor recreation in the countryside is examined in Chapters 5 and 6. Their limited success is largely explained by their failure to promote the range of recreational environments and social settings most people seek when out in the countryside and by their failure to address the recreational needs of particular groups in society. This appraisal also points to the inertia represented by the cultural legacy of a pattern of sites inherited from earlier periods and traditional approaches to management which serve to conserve particular kinds of environments rather than public enjoyment of them and to thereby protect private landed interests.

More recent countryside recreation policies based on 'partnership initiatives' (Chapter 7) reflect not only attempts by the public sector to overcome this inertia by linking recreation to a general programme of environmental improvement and education, but they also reflect the new set of social, economic and political circumstances portended by the worsening economy of the 1970s and to the reassertion of a free-market economy adhered to throughout the 1980s by a Conservative government.

There is common agreement that the 1980s proved to be a period of profound social, economic and political change in Britain, but there is rather less agreement about whether these changes have affected environmental values and countryside recreation in particular. By the end of the 1970s both economic growth and growth in countryside recreation had slowed down. But, while the proportion of the population who visited the countryside for informal recreation remained fairly stable (Countryside Commission, 1986, OPCS, 1988), the pattern of growth exhibited in water sports was spectacular and other outdoor acitivities like motor sports and water sports continued to grow at a steady rate (Centre for Leisure Research, 1986). Neither the straitened economic circumstances of the period nor a new political environment seemed to account very readily for these shifts. Equally problematic was the reluctance of non-participants in outdoor recreation to respond to public policies designed to raise their participation rates. Amongst the unemployed, participation in sports declined during a period when the Sports Council deliberately pursued a policy to encourage them to participate (McIntosh and Charlton, 1985) and the proportion of other non-participating groups such as households with young families and people without access to a car, remained predictably low.

Significantly too, the proportion of the population with no recent tradition of visiting the countryside remained remarkably consistent during a twenty year period during which policies designed to improve the accessibility of the countryside had been pursued. At a time of rising unemployment, such evidence did indeed suggest that some reassessment of public recreation policies was required and especially of those policies designed to raise participation amongst the community as a whole. The election of a Conservative government, dedicated to the pursuit of a free-market economy, ensured that this reassessment would take place against the background of a new social, economic and political order in which socially-motivated policies would not find favour.

The final chapter of the book attempts to place countryside recreation in its contemporary social and cultural setting by drawing on studies which have tried to link changing social attitudes to leisure behaviour. Some suggestions are made about the way in which contemporary society is challenging conventional views about the appropriate recreational use of the countryside and about the role the public sector might play in countryside recreation.

Theories of countryside recreation and the evidence available

One of the central tenets of this study is that it is not possible to understand what role countryside recreation plays in modern society without also looking at how people live out their lives; that is, it is important to position countryside recreation in relation to employment and work practices, household structures, gender relations, mobility, leisure time and locality. It is also important to place people's enjoyment of the countryside in the wider context of those social relations which govern access to the environments people seek; namely proprietorial rights and free-market mechanisms for gaining access to the countryside. Without this perspective it is not possible to determine what countryside recreation has come to mean in modern society.

In order to achieve these objectives the study takes as its starting point theories of leisure which combine an understanding of attitudes to the countryside with studies of changes in the social context within which recreation takes place (Chapter 1). The need for such an approach has been demonstrated by several studies, most notably those of Williams (1975), Thomas (1984) and Pepper (1984). Williams shows that the countryside is a powerful evocation of a way of life which contrasts favourably with the utilitarian and materialistic values manifest in urban life. He also shows through an analysis of poetry, literature and art how this dialectic relationship has evolved in complex ways over time. Pepper's study too reveals that much of the diversity which characterizes the modern environmental movement reflects differing attitudes to man and nature, to determinism and free-will philosophies and to different modes of political action. Why people place such a high value on the countryside is thus intimately bound up with social and cultural aspects of everyday life. Disentangling this complex relationship is difficult but, by drawing on the combined results of quantitative and qualitative social surveys, the book seeks to provide an analysis which acknowledges directly, both the social and cultural roots of countryside recreation.

Like recent studies of women's leisure (Green et al., 1987) and the comprehensive study of access to the countryside for recreation and sport (Countryside Commission, 1986), questionnaire surveys based on the responses of householders or visitors to countryside sites and recreation facilities are used here to describe people's recreational behaviour. Since 1977 the National Survey of Countryside Recreation has provided a national picture of informal outdoor recreation and the General Household Survey also provides valuable information on participation rates in walking and other sports. Several regional and sub-regional studies undertaken in the 1970s also provide information on expressed demand through interviews conducted at sites in the countryside for example the Study of Informal Recreation in the South East (SIRSEE), (Elson and Sienkiewicz, 1977), Leisure in the North West (Patmore and Rogers, 1972) and Harrison (1983). These quantitative studies reveal the popularity of countryside recreation amongst the population as a whole and the relative popularity of different recreational activities, environments and facilities.

Qualitative studies are used here as a means of understanding people's motivations for engaging in outdoor recreation and for identifying different attitudes and values. Examples of these studies are provided by the work of Mostyn (1979) who examined the personal benefits people gained from participating in conservation projects on open spaces, group discussions convened by the Qualitative Consultancy (1986) on behalf of the Countryside Commission to enquire into peoples motivations behind visiting the countryside, and work conducted by the author in collaboration with colleagues into popular values for open space and the countryside (Harrison et al., 1986). These studies suggest that the countryside is enjoyed for a wide range of reasons and that pleasure is derived from experiencing many diverse physical and social settings. They also provide insights into the relationship between environmental values and social class, gender and ethnicity.

As a means of demonstrating how countryside recreation is socially constructed through the way society is organized and culturally constructed through the differing values placed on the countryside over time, Chapter 1 positions countryside recreation within the broad field of leisure studies and leisure theory. Arguments used to advocate state involvement in countryside recreation are then seen to reflect, not only differing views about the importance of leisure in society, but also differing views about how and why the countryside is enjoyed. In this way the foundations of the study are established and recreation is approached, not as a set of economic activities and land-uses but, as the expression of deeply-entrenched, social and cultural ideals.

1

Countryside recreation, leisure and the state

....

Introduction

Countryside recreation defies easy categorization as an arena of human activity – it is part sport, part socializing and part relaxing and visits to the countryside involve a wide range of activities, experiences and emotions. This complexity means that it is difficult to provide a single unifying theory of countryside recreation even within the broad framework provided by leisure studies. But it is as a form of leisure activity that countryside recreation is enjoyed and it is to leisure theories that we must look for explanations of its popularity in Britain. At the outset however, several aspects of countryside recreation set it apart from other kinds of leisure activity.

First, unlike many leisure pursuits undertaken away from the home, the environmental setting in which recreation takes place is an integral part of the leisure experience. Countryside recreation can only take place in the countryside and not anywhere else. Having access to favoured environments in the countryside is thus crucial to the leisure experience. But in England and Wales, the public do not have a right of access to the countryside – save that legislated for as Public Rights of Way and other Access Areas negotiated by the state and land owners. In consequence the countryside is not a free good available to all; rather it is a positional or scarce good available first and foremost to those who own the land and those able to pay for access to it when the landlord sees fit. Where, when and what recreation takes place in the countryside is thus determined by the bundle of rights landlords acquire through property ownership.

So central are private property rights to British society that it is not possible to understand what countryside recreation means in modern society without addressing their importance. As a result, not only has countryside recreation become 'organized' through the establishment of associations and membership groups but, organized groups have had to demonstrate that they would conduct themselves responsibly before successful access to the countryside could be negotiated with landlords. In other words countryside recreation has become defined through law *and* custom and the State has proved reluctant to alter this position.

Second, the extent to which people can gain access to preferred environments is determined not only by their willingness to join organizations but by other personal circumstances as well eg: owning a car, proximity to the countryside, knowledge of locations etc. It is also influenced by the extent to which public rights of access exist in the countryside itself ie. supply. Visitor patterns and behaviour are therefore likely to be a poor indicator of potential demand and will disguise the true extent of latent demand. Under these circumstances the state might be expected to intervene on grounds of social equity much as it has done for recreational provision in the urban area where standards of provision and open space hierarchies have been used as 'norms' and guides for determining desirable levels of public facilities (Veal, 1987). But history reveals that the state has not regarded countryside recreation as a right of citizenship or as a basic statutory requirement of local government, preferring instead to regard it as a discretionary function to be provided as and when public authorities see fit.

Third, and somewhat more problematic, is the assumption that countryside and its enjoyment mean the same thing to everyone. History reveals that attitudes to the countryside have changed over time but a dominant ideology of the countryside has prevailed amongst landowners, professionals and the public sector throughout the post-war period. This ideology, here called the *countryside aesthetic*, portrays the countryside as fine landscape and its appropriate enjoyment as being achieved through solitary and quiet pursuits. By exercising this ideology in public debates about countryside recreation, private landed interests have ensured that their interests have been served well and the state has been prevailed upon to adopt a residuary role in countryside recreation rather than an instrumental one (Blunden and Curry, 1989). In consequence, the demands of non-conforming recreational uses have not been met (Elson, Buller and Stanley, 1987) and access to the wider countryside has not been extended (Shoard, 1987).

Lastly, any theory of countryside recreation would have to account for the phenomenal growth of these activities over the post-war period – especially the increase in informal visits to the farmed and settled countryside. In part this growth mirrors a general rise in the standard of living across the social spectrum, but why affluence should result in visits to the countryside rather than to the coast or abroad also needs to be explained. At the same time, the popularity accorded to the countryside might be regarded as part of the wider environmental movement experienced by all industrialized nations in the post-war period. Viewed as part of this environmental movement, visits to the countryside become a means of experiencing the better world the countryside represents. In a nation that has been urbanized longer than any others in the industrialized world, visits become a tangible expression of deeply-held cultural values. Countryside recreation is then less an expression of people's material circumstances but of their emotional and spiritual values as well, and rising affluence alone cannot adequately explain the high regard in which the countryside is held.

Having access to the countryside and being able to enjoy it where, when and how people wish, is thus intimately bound up with people's social ideals and the kind of society people aspire to. Whether or not the state should intervene to secure the extensive access some ideals suggest, depends crucially upon how leisure itself is defined and valued and the position leisure occupies in the kind of society people want. As later chapters will show, the extent to which the state has intervened in countryside recreation in England and Wales has depended not only upon its reluctance to compromise the proprietorial rights of private landed interests but also on its reluctance to see countryside recreation as little more than a luxury to be provided on a discretionary basis. In the section which follows, an attempt is made to show how these aspects of countryside recreation impinge on theories of leisure and state involvement.

Theories of leisure

Leisure as a right of citizenship

With its origins in classical Greek society, this theory proposes that an acceptable society is one in which all its citizens benefit from the opportunity to engage in a variety of leisure pursuits. Utopian views of society especially prevalent in the late nineteenth and early twentieth centuries embrace this concept – many of them using model rural communities as their ideal. Through the writings of William Morris and others (see Williams, 1975) social reform and the establishment of an egalitarian society is linked to communal modes of production with many such communes established in rural settings. But even Utopian idealists are not agreed about what form leisure would take in these ideal societies. For example, Veal (1988) notes that a life

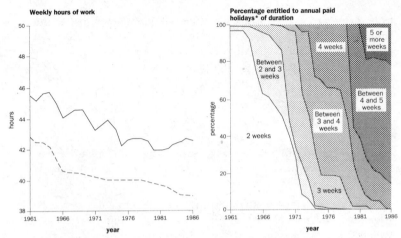

* The information related to basic entitlements in national collective agreements or Wages Council Orders

Figure 1.1: Trends in hours of work and holiday entitlement 1961–86
Source: HMSO, 1988

devoted to the hedonistic pursuit of play was not acceptable to either Howard (1898) or Joad (1935), both influential thinkers who sought to fuse ideas about an ideal society with planning as an instrument for guiding social and environmental change. In practice, because there is little agreement about what form leisure opportunities might take, it is also difficult to justify why or how the state might become involved in promoting or securing such a society.

In a capitalistic society based on private enterprise such as Britain, legislation designed to restrict the number of hours worked and to establish national holidays is one means of ensuring wide social benefits. Even then, Britain still enjoys fewer public holidays than many of its European neighbours and, since first introducing legislation designed to secure paid holiday entitlement for employees in the mid-twentieth century, the state has preferred to leave decisions about additional holiday entitlement in the hands of employers. Over that intervening period, British trade unions have consistently pursued a shorter working-week and paid holiday entitlement for their workers rather than necessarily maximizing wages. In choosing this strategy they argue that such increases bring wide benefits to society as a whole, not just to employees. Figure 1.1 testifies to the success of these negotiations and illustrates how the period since 1960 has seen a substantial increase in the number of employees benefiting from paid holiday entitlement (HMSO, 1988) and an overall reduction in the normal basic hours worked. It could be argued that in the absence

4

of trade unions, employers might be expected to seek improvements in productivity through extending the working week rather than reducing it, so in broad terms the negotiating strategy adopted by unions appears to have brought substantial gains.

Determining whether or not 'money in the pocket' could have achieved these same benefits is less easy. Studies by Roberts (1978) on the leisure lives of low paid workers suggest that this indeed might be the case although Wilson (1988) suggests that the British attitude to work is also a distinctive one. Compared with their European neighbours, British workers are satisficers rather than optimizers when it comes to conditions of employment and the pursuit by the unions of a reduction in the hours worked rather than maximization of wages can be regarded an expression of deeply-held beliefs and attitudes to life in general rather than to work or leisure in particular. Equally, demonstrating that this optimizing strategy is an effective and efficient means of achieving a leisured society begs the question of how a leisured society might be recognized. In the absence of any agreement about what form society might take or what place leisure might occupy in it, it is easy to see why in a capitalist society based on private enterprise, successive national governments have been happy to treat leisure as 'time not spent at work' and hence to be determined as part of the wage-bargaining process – not as a basic right of citizenship like education and health.

Leisure as the antithesis of work

The central position of paid employment in the lives of most adults in the industrialized world means that it is tempting to define leisure as time not spent in work. Activities undertaken out of work then become classified as leisure activities – including presumably travelling to and from the workplace. Defined in this way, some individuals and groups in society who are not employed – children and young people, full-time housewives and elderly people – have a life replete with leisure even though their own experiences suggest otherwise (Figure 1.2). So, defining leisure in relation to work provides only a partial answer to the question of what people themselves mean by leisure and how they experience it. Modifying this definition to exclude time spent on activities essential to the maintenance and reproduction of the household helps to highlight the differing social and economic responsibilities men and women have in society. Taken together, time spent in activities such as cooking, cleaning and do-it-yourself, caring for children and dependent relatives as well as socializing with them, means that many people in modern society have little 'free' or 'unallocated' time – even if they are not fully employed.

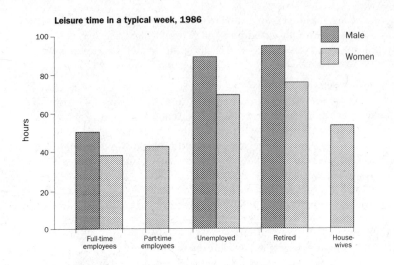

Leisure time in a typical week, 1986

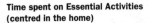

**Time spent on Essential Activities
(centred in the home)**

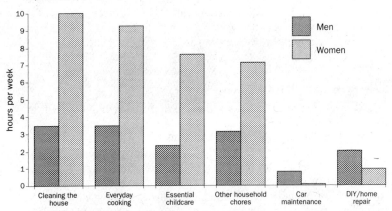

Figure 1.2: Leisure time, time use and occupational status
Source: The Henley Centre for Forecasting

Moreover, people living in households where one or more members are employed in shift-work may find that these windows of unallocated time seldom coincide with other members of the household or those of their friends. As a result their leisure time may prove to be unusable except for solitary pursuits.

Studies of work practices in some modern industries suggest that there is a tendency for employers to favour 24 hour shifts as a means of improving efficiency and output. One result of this trend is an increase in the numbers of shift-workers who experience an increase in unsociable hours and an erosion of usable leisure time (Sports Council, 1986). Likewise, other studies have shown that many women experience lives which are closely circumscribed by their household responsibilities (Stockdale, 1985). Activity diaries kept by men and women in the same household illustrate how 'leisure-poor' many women's lives are in comparison to those of their partner and a recent study of women's leisure (Green et al., 1987) reveals that women who are single-parents lead especially constrained lives. Only by calling on an extended social network, often involving complex negotiations with third parties, can single parents secure 'unallocated time' in which to be at leisure. The growing number of single-person households with children or dependent relatives in Britain further suggests that the proportion of people who are likely to regard themselves as having little or no leisure will also increase. Defined in this way, leisure is socially constructed not only in relation to modes of economic organization and work practices but also in relation to the roles society expects men and women to play in it.

In the context of countryside recreation, the popularity of weekends for undertaking visits to the countryside emphasizes the importance of extended periods of shared or common time in which groups of family and friends can enjoy themselves together. Legislation designed to regulate working practices and shop hours has contributed to the emergence of the weekend in Britain as the most readily identifiable time period for engaging in leisure activities – especially those motivated by socialising. At the same time, changes in wider social attitudes have been important too. So for example, the decline in the importance of religious beliefs which traditionally regarded Sunday as a day devoted to religious activities, has meant that even without changes in work and school hours, changing social attitudes have played an important role in influencing how usable leisure time is defined.

Defining leisure in relation to work and the constraints on usable time imposed by household structure, thus provides only a partial explanation of differential participation rates in leisure activities such as visiting the countryside. It does serve to highlight the fact that some people may never have the extended blocks of time needed to get out to the countryside. For those people who reside far away from the countryside and do not have access to a car, visiting the countryside may never be a practical possibility particularly when journeys by

Table 1.1: Time use in a typical week: by economic status and sex, 1989
Source: Henley Centre for Forecasting

| | Full-time employees | | Part-time employees | | |
	Males	Females	Females	Housewives	Retired
Weekly hours spent on:					
Employment and travel (1)	48.9	43.6	21.0	0.4	0.7
Essential activities (2)	25.9	42.2	58.6	65.3	30.8
Sleep (3)	49.0	49.0	49.0	49.0	49.0
Free time	44.2	33.2	39.4	53.3	87.5
Free time per weekday	4.7	3.2	4.7	7.1	12.3
Free time per weekend day	10.4	8.5	8.0	9.0	13.1

(1) Travel to and from place of work
(2) Essential domestic work and personal care. Including essential shopping, child care, cooking, washing and getting up and going to bed
(3) An average of 7 hours sleep per night is assumed

public transport take a long time. Such theories do suggest however, that countryside recreation like other leisure forms is socially constructed both by the differing constraints on time that result from the position households occupy in the economy and from the roles men and women are expected to play in particular households. They also help to explain which groups in society are unlikely to participate in countryside recreation; for example, people living in low income households, in households where members are on shift work and in households with young children and dependent relatives whose members cannot call upon a social network of friends or relatives to help them negotiate free time.

Defining and studying leisure in terms of unallocated time rather than time not spent at work thus reinforces how leisure-poor are the lives of some people and social groups in the population (Table 1.1). It also suggests that to be fully effective, socially-motivated policies designed to improve the leisure lives of particular groups in society would need to address these wider structural changes in society rather than to concentrate on recreational provision per se. That successive governments have preferred not to address the question of leisure poverty in this way is a measure of the pervasive influence of the economic structure of society on leisure itself. But, these social explanations do not fully account for the comparative popularity of the countryside as the preferred destination of the overwhelming majority of leisure trips undertaken away from the home. Neither do they explain why people who are constrained by both time and resources aspire to visit the countryside more often. In other words, any socially based theory of countryside recreation which ignores the immense appeal of the countryside as a highly valued leisure environment is likely to underestimate the cultural roots of countryside recreation.

Leisure and life-enhancement

Linked with ideas of the rational recreation movement of the nineteenth century in Britain, this theory proposes that idle time is wasted time but time devoted to appropriate activities is productive and life-enhancing. Defining those activities which are deemed to be appropriate however, involves both matters of taste and judgement and within the field of leisure activities some activities have consistently been deemed to be more appropriate than others. As Veal (1988) notes, drinking and gambling for example are regarded as inappropriate both because they are seen to encourage licentious behaviour and to lead to moral depravity. By contrast, intellectual activities such as admiring fine landscape or paintings are regarded as morally and spiritually uplifting. Equally, participation in organized team sports is deemed to be appropriate because it fosters a corporate spirit and proper behaviour. Hence it is argued, time spent on appropriate leisure activities contributes to a healthy and reliable work-force, to a fit and well-drilled defence force and to a general improvement in moral standards and social behaviour.

The 'moral affluence' of this argument appealed to a number of prominent people in Victorian society (Bailey, 1978). Politicians, civic dignitaries and philanthropists regarded town parks, libraries and museums as a means of enhancing the lives of the urban poor and in a similar vein, the founding members of the National Trust acquired countryside sites close to the edge of cities for 'the benefit of public enjoyment'. Inherent in such an approach are accusations of paternalism and rationalism. By imposing the attitudes and values of a dominant group or class in society on subordinate ones, a particular social and economic structure is perpetuated at the expense of a new order. Well-intentioned motives and messianic zeal amount to little more than misplaced philanthropy if the real needs of those who are thought to benefit are neither questioned nor researched. In other words, to promote the acquisition of open spaces for the use of the public without also improving housing, education and health is to ignore the real condition of the poor and its causes. Furthermore, by restricting particular activities from taking place on these public open spaces through the imposition of by-laws – for example, by prohibiting overnight camping, the playing of music and ball games, a particular kind of contemplative and intellectualized enjoyment of the countryside is promoted that meshes well with notions of moral affluence valued by those educated people who occupy positions of power and authority in society.

The many initiatives taken by metropolitan authorities and charitable trusts to improve public access to open spaces both in the towns and countryside during the nineteenth and twentieth centuries were often promoted as a means of enhancing the lives of the poor, but the supposed relationship between these environmental improvements and social reform were hard to demonstrate. People were not necessarily happier as a result of having open spaces to visit, neither did they acquire a new sense of purpose nor did they necessarily act as more responsible citizens. Notwithstanding the difficulty of proving the correctness of this 'rational' argument, the concept of 'appropriate recreational use' of the countryside has played and continues to play a dominant role in shaping environmental legislation, recreational policy and attitudes to the leisure use of the countryside in Britain. Later chapters will show how this concept above all others has been used to both promote the enjoyment of the countryside as a life-enhancing activity and as means of protecting the dominant interests in the countryside – those of private landowners.

Leisure as a luxury

The notion that leisure is a luxury only to be engaged in once basic needs have been satisfied begs the question 'What are basic needs?' (Mercer, 1973). In so far as human beings have biological needs, then basic needs include warmth, shelter, clothing and food, otherwise life cannot be sustained. Evidence from the most traditional of societies shows that these needs can be catered for without recourse to sophisticated levels of technological development, so the question of whether or not leisure is a basic need also arises. Adherents to the view that leisure is a luxury to be engaged in when and where people wish to, argue that the state has no role to play in leisure provision and such a view will always find some acceptance in society. But, of relevance to an explanation of the post-war rise of environmentalism and the parallel rise in popularity of countryside recreation is Maslow's theory of a hierarchy of needs and its development by Inglehart (1977).

According to Maslow's theory (Maslow, 1969), once basic needs are satisfied then people aspire to satisfy other needs especially those in short supply. Characteristically these are self-actualization needs – the need for self-esteem, the need to belong and a variety of post-material needs relating to a concern for the quality of life rather than with material rewards. Regarded in this light the popularity accorded to countryside conservation and recreation is one expression of these post-material needs. The priority given by a post-war generation to post-material needs is regarded by Inglehart as a pre-requisite for the rise of environmentalism. He suggests that the roots of a marked generational shift towards post-material values amongst people who grew up in the post-war period can be attributed to the experience of affluence in adolescence.

Like Maslow, Inglehart assumes that the differential support for post-material values at times of affluence relates to the higher value placed on those needs in shortest supply – post-material ones. As more young people experience affluence in adolescence, the general direction values in society will take is towards post-material values. Overall, there is sufficient evidence to suggest that the general trajectory followed by changes in social attitudes towards the environment supports this theory. For example a recent survey of social attitudes in Britain (Young, 1989) reports growing concern about environmental issues, including undesirable changes in the countryside and cross cultural comparisons also demonstrate a growth in public concern for the environment (Commission of the European Communities, 1987). Viewed in this way visits to the countryside can be regarded as the actualization of deeply-felt needs especially those relating to the high quality of life associated with the countryside – increased prosperity and car-ownership the means of achieving them.

Inglehart's theory however, does not explain why some people and groups in society place a stronger emphasis on post-material values than others. The theory suggests that all people are motivated by the same set of needs and that these needs are satisfied in a particular order. In other words by concentrating on economic affluence as the means of satisfying needs, the needs theory neglects other influences on human behaviour and social attitudes. Cotgrove and Duff (1981) and other workers in America such as Van Liere and Dunlap (1980) and Buttel and Johnson (1977) suggest that human behaviour is not always 'needs-satisficing'; it is also 'goal-orientated'. Values are then associated with ideals not just needs and in cases where ideals also have political expression, how ideals are politicized in the home and in people's 'life-styles' can also influence adolescents (Veal, 1989).

Cotgrove and Duff's study of the social ideals of four different social groups – industrialists, trade-unionists, members of environmental organizations and members of the general public, found that the ideological basis of support for post-material values varied widely between the groups. Even after controlling for age, senior industrialists are significantly more materialistic than members of the public, and environmentalists are much more post-materialistic. Furthermore, these authors note 'the shift towards post-materialism in younger age groups is small by comparison with between-group differences' (p.93) and the experience of affluence in adolescence on its own is not sufficient to explain inter-generational differences in post-material values or their social distribution. Moreover, Inglehart's thesis does not allow for the fact that attitudes may change during later life. In a society where the mass media play an important role in raising people's awareness of environmental issues including change in the countryside, it seems rather simplistic to assume that the experience of affluence alone, is the root cause of value shifts even within the leisure field (Burgess, 1990).

Cotgrove and Duff (1981) conclude that sources of changing environmental and social values are complex and stem from the multiple influences of changes in the structure of modern industrial societies and the differential experiences of those who occupy various positions in the social structure. Likewise, as the behavioural expression of deeply-held, environmental values, participation in outdoor recreation in the countryside is likely to reflect socially and culturally related ideals not merely the indulgence of a prosperous society.

Countryside recreation and state involvement

A review of theories of leisure shows that it is difficult to position countryside recreation within a single conceptual framework (Bernard, 1983), although theories informed by both social and attitudinal changes seem more appropriate than others for explaining the rise and popularity of countryside recreation in Britain. Against this background it is also clear that the rationales used to justify state involvement in countryside recreation in Britain throughout the modern period owe more to arguments based on moral affluence first advocated in the Victorian period than they do to arguments based on ideals of good citizenship (see Chapters 2 and 3). But underlying this argument too is an acceptance of the dominance of proprietorial rights. As long as private property rights remain central to the way British society is organized, public access to the countryside can only be secured on an extensive basis, either through state ownership of land or by the state negotiating with landowners on behalf of the public. So central is the position of proprietorial rights to British society that even public access to common land outside the metropolitan area is not a legal right and, unlike some Scandinavian countries, the right of any citizen to wander across another's property, does not exist.

At the same time, intervention by the state to protect fine countryside areas and access to them, such as National Parks legislation, has been enacted over land already settled and farmed. Such action has always met prolonged and fierce opposition from private landed interests (Blunden and Curry, 1989). Unlike many European countries and North America which still possess substantial tracts of wild and unsettled country and where National Parks are truly national, environmental and recreational legislation in Britain has not succeeded in compromising the interests of private landlords to any marked extent. Countryside recreation therefore, remains severely constrained and influenced by private property rights.

Whether or not the state should intervene to alter the inviolability of private property rights as Shoard (1987) has argued, is ultimately a question of political ideals and the kind of society such actions are designed to achieve. In the past, proponents of such action have not been able to agree what form such a society would take and there is every reason to believe this is still true today, so strongly entrenched in British society are private landed interests. Even if the state chooses not to legislate for changes in the rights of private land ownership but chooses instead to enter the land market directly, intervention in a free-market economy will always be restricted by the costs of land acquisition and considerations of compensation to private land owners.

Other questions also arise. For example, should the state intervene to purchase extensive countryside tracts irrespective of how accessible they are to the majority of the population? Should the finest landscapes be preserved or ordinary countryside as well? Should the state intervene to increase the accessibility of the countryside by subsidizing public transport or, should the state provide selective support for recreational activities in the countryside by funding events and facilities designed to appeal to particular groups of people? And, over what time scale should these subsidies prevail? In the final analysis the extent of state involvement is likely to depend crucially upon demonstrating the benefits to society as a whole. Because it is difficult to substantiate precisely what these benefits are, state intervention is always likely to remain a question of social and political ideals.

Conclusion

The history of countryside recreation in Britain presented in Chapters 2 and 3 reveals that the state has been reluctant to play an instrumental role in countryside recreation and although from time to time it has intervened to protect areas of fine landscape from development and to promote public access to particular areas through the operation of Rights of Way legislation, Access and Management Agreements and the establishment of Country Parks, these facilitating measures have done little to alter the dominant influence of private property interests (Sheial, 1981, Blunden and Curry, 1989). Rather, as Cherry (1975) observes, the state has reacted to external situations by seeking to balance the positions of affected interest groups and has seldom intervened on behalf of countryside recreation interests. In practice, as the following chapters will show, a powerful alliance between landed interests, environmentalists and rural local authorities gained ground throughout the twentieth century and together they were often aligned *against* recreationalists. Sharing a common ideology of the countryside and its appropriate recreational use – the countryside aesthetic – this alliance has been able to put sufficient pressure on the state to ensure that the balance of interest continues to lie with landowners. Through successful lobbying of parliament at times when new legislation appeared to threaten proprietorial interests, rural landowners exerted a particularly powerful influence (Cherry, 1985). As a result where people go in the countryside, what activities they can take part in and when they can take place is severely constrained both by custom and by law.

Only now, as we approach the end of the century, is there a reworking of this alliance because the agricultural imperative which guided land-use decisions in the countryside has been challenged. For the first time since the last war landowners have begun to regard countryside recreation as an economic activity in its own right. As they reassess their capital assets in the face of declining returns from agriculture, new forms of outdoor leisure have begun to test the countryside aesthetic and new residents are beginning to assert their influence on how the countryside is used and protected. Not for the first time in the history of countryside recreation, the scene is set for a contest of countryside ideologies. But, unlike earlier disputes, for example in the 1930s and 1960s, many more people in society are now both users and protectors of the countryside. The extent to which contemporary society will be able to forge a new recreational relationship with the countryside will depend upon whether the countryside aesthetic remains the dominant ideology. The main purpose of succeeding chapters is to show how this dominant ideology has played such a potent role in determining what countryside recreation has come to mean in modern society.

2

Trends in outdoor recreation and provision: Up to 1960

....

Introduction

As we start the last decade of the twentieth century we take very much for granted the fact that the countryside plays a key role in our recreation and it seems unthinkable that this has not always been the case. But, in practice it is to the Victorian era that we must turn to begin to understand why countryside recreation has achieved the popularity it is currently accorded (Thomas, 1984, Shoard, 1987 and Sheail, 1981). During this period, not only did the numbers of people who engaged in countryside pursuits increase, but people's attitudes to the countryside also changed in ways that have now become accepted as common place. In much the same way that Williams (1975) and Thomas (1984) have shown how changing attitudes to the country and the natural world reflect what people think of themselves and the society they live in, so too we must recognise that these kinds of relationships influence how countryside recreation is defined and what it means. They impinge on the way in which demand for countryside recreation is expressed and on the activities and actions of those agencies, planners, professionals and individuals who are in a position to influence demand and its spatial, environmental and social effects. In order to understand the place that the wider countryside occupies in our leisure activities, we need to study the official history of events *and* to examine how both values and attitudes to the countryside and its leisure use have changed.

The purpose of this chapter is to review trends in countryside recreation and provision as a basis for revealing how attitudes to the countryside and its recreational use have changed over time. The chapter examines the issues and actions which predominated during four time periods up to 1960 and explores the values and concepts underpinning them. It shows that many of the actions taken in the public arena were designed to influence how and where the countryside could be enjoyed. It shows too that these actions served to promote a particular ideology of the countryside in which the quiet contemplative appreciation of fine landscapes was regarded as the most appropriate way of enjoying the countryside – an ideology which subsequently came to occupy a prominent position in public sector policies for countryside recreation.

The early period 1800–1920

The transformation of British society during the early part of the Victorian era from a rural society in which four out of five people lived in the country at the end of the eighteenth century, to an urban society in which one in two lived in a town by 1830, saw major changes in people's attitudes to the natural world as well as in people's place of residence, the quality of their immediate environment and their leisure time. During this period as Thomas shows, (Thomas, 1984), the monolithic view of the natural world as one of divine creation and as one subservient to the uses of mankind was supplanted by a new range of attitudes. For the first time many educated people became aware that the earth and its wildlife had an existence independent of human beings and people from all walks of life came to delight in the diversity of nature and in its study. The establishment of zoological and botanical gardens dates from this period as do natural history museums and societies. In the urban area, the practice of including small zoos in public parks reflected the intrinsic appeal of animals, whether wild, domesticated, exotic or familiar. Many people came to accept that wildlife could and should co-exist quite happily with humankind and so came to question the correctness of the prevailing attitude to nature, which until then had been one of domination, subjugation and profligacy.

These new-found attitudes to the natural world based on custodianship, companionship and scientific enquiry co-existed with other more utilitarian attitudes. Victorian society was dedicated to industrial and imperial expansion, and international commerce and trade flourished. Towns and cities grew apace engulfing the countryside as they expanded. Between 1821 and 1841 London grew by 20% but the northern industrial towns grew faster – Manchester, Birmingham, Leeds and Sheffield by more than 40% and Bradford by 65%. For many city residents the countryside became farther away, both in space and in time as the towns and cities came to be populated by successive generations of 'townies'. But importantly too, the role that the countryside played in peoples lives and their imaginations also changed. By the 1880s, when the British economy began to enter a period of relative decline, the values of enlightenment and improvement which extolled the virtues of the city as a civilizing and beneficial influence on society were being questioned. Housing conditions of the urban poor were appalling, insanitary conditions and polluted water supplies meant disease was rife, and the air above cities was polluted with smoke and chemicals. Faced with such potent evidence of the damaging effects of unbridled economic growth, many educated people came to regard the countryside as a repository for their dreams and yearnings – a Golden Age that represented all that the city was not.

Through the writings of the times Williams traces how complex were the views of the city and the country during the nineteenth century; cities were alternately regarded as both liberating and alienating. Views which were counterposed with those of the country which was mocked for the 'idiocy' of country life and extolled for its ' knowable communities'. Williams (1975) shows how a rapidly changing social order generated by industrialization and urbanization spawned new and often contradictory attitudes to the country, the city, nature and the mass of humanity. Furthermore, contradictory attitudes to leisure and leisure activities abounded. Pleasure gardens, like Vauxhall Gardens, which had been patronised by rich and poor alike were closed, partly to make way for urban development and partly to be replaced by model parks that permitted only appropriate and restrained leisure behaviour. Moral and aesthetic reform became linked together in the activities of social reformers of the times such as Octavia Hill and George Shaw Lefevre who recognised the importance of open space for even the poorest of workers. They and others set about not only improving housing conditions but also preserving open space for access by all citizens. Moreover, it was argued that by experiencing leisure environments most sought after by the middle and upper classes, the urban poor would come to share these same leisure tastes and values.

The defence of urban commons and the public open space movement of this period has been interpreted as part of a wider social movement which rejected the prevailing materialistic values of Victorian free-enterprise. The so-called 'rational recreation movement' propounded by social reformers of the mid-nineteenth century advocated more open space provision in the city in the belief that the provision of facilities for respectable recreation such as public walks, libraries and museums, would imbue the working classes with the values of the middle classes (Bailey, 1978). They argued that improvements in the

17

physical and moral welfare of the working classes would be achieved and as a result, social unrest could be contained. But, the defence of the urban commons that was mounted during this period by social reformers and certain municipal authorities, served as a symbol of other values as well. In much the same way that the traditional countryside had become a repository for people dreams and aspirations for a better way of life, so too the urban commons represented all that was good about a pre-industrial and even pre-feudal economy in which communal rights prevailed over those of private ownership (Lowe and Goyder, 1983). Prompted by the action of several landowners who had begun to enclose commonlands and by a report of a parliamentary select committee, the government of the day set about intervening to protect commons and obtain land for public recreation. Between 1836 and 1845 general enclosure acts made provision for the preservation of commons within 16 km of Charing Cross in London, but in the case of Hampstead Heath and other commons such as Epping Forest, neither the effective municipal government (Metropolitan Board of Works) or the national government was prepared to intervene to prevent development. It was to defend commons from the avaricious intentions of Lords' of the Manor that in 1865 George Lefevre founded the Commons Preservation Society so as to restore to the commons 'something of the attributes of the ancient Saxon Folk-land.' (1894)

By contrast the several people's parks which were funded by private donation and municipal enterprise during this period, contained more formal environments and reflected both utilitarian approaches to the use of public open space and a discipline to leisure behaviour that was at odds with the essentially communal nature of the resource (Cunningham, 1980,). Acts of Parliament enabled some of the most famous of Victorian parks to be established in London at a time when demand for housing, industry and commerce were high. But whilst some parks such as Victoria (1841) and Battersea Park (1844), were accessible to those most in need of open space, Southwood Park (1857) and Finsbury Park (1860) were located in suburbs inhabited by the better-off workers. Moreover, the range of facilities and environments they offered reflected a disciplined and restrained approach to public enjoyment that conflicted with the essentially social nature of the leisure pursuits enjoyed by the working classes of the time. The playing of games, consumption of alcohol, playing of music or holding meetings were either prohibited in these parks or strictly controlled. By comparison, the more naturalistic environments of the urban commons such as Hampstead Heath and Wimbledon Common provided a symbol of open countryside and a setting for traditional pastimes and spontaneous socializing reminiscent of rural life.

Neither urban commons nor municipal parks on their own could satisfy the demand for outdoor recreation partly because of the nature of recreation they were able to offer and partly because the pressure to develop open land in the urban area meant that their distribution was uneven. Philanthropists and social reformers alike looked to the countryside on the edge of major towns and cities to provide sites which could be preserved and opened up for public access. One of the most celebrated victories of this period was the acquisition of Epping Forest by the City of London Corporation for enjoyment by the people of London. Spurred by events in adjacent Hainault Forest where the Crown Commissioners had enclosed the wood- pasture and converted it to farmland, the Corporation set about securing commoners' rights to Epping Forest and contested all encroachments and piecemeal enclosures in the courts. In 1878, the Epping Forest Act transferred the freehold of the Forest to the City Corporation who were charged with the responsibility of appointing conservators to manage it as public open space. This victory coupled with the extension of working class suburbia as far out as Edmonton, Tottenham, Walthamstow and Leyton meant that the forest became a popular destination for outings by all classes. A cheap fare agreement entered into by the Great Eastern Railway Company in 1864 enabled passengers to travel at low fares for up to 16 km on some of its suburban lines and by 1883 all railways were obliged by the Cheap Trains Act to offer special workmen's fares. In consequence not only were the better-off workers enabled to move to London's suburbs but recreational travel also became a real possibility for those left behind nearer the city centre. Layton's (1985) attempt to reconstruct the recreational use of the Forest from various contemporary accounts of the times, shows that indeed Epping Forest had its hey-day in this period (Table 2.1).

The Corporation also secured other properties around London for use as public open space such as Burnham Beeches, Kenley Common and Banstead and Coulsdon Commons and their activities were soon complimented by those of other organizations such as the National Trust founded in 1895. The Trust was originally founded in response to the growing pressures from development in northern Surrey and western Kent and sought to acquire land either by gift or purchase. Octavia Hill, a founder member, had worked to secure better housing conditions for London's poor and was committed to the idea of securing access to natural areas which could benefit all citizens. By acquiring land for this purpose, several sites around London were saved from development for example Box Hill and Ivinghoe Beacon. But, the Trust became devoted to preserving the natural landscapes much favoured by the intelligentsia, like the Lake District and these were often remote from centres of population and inaccessible save to those

Table 2.1: Estimates of visitor numbers in Epping Forest
Source: Layton, 1985

Date	Area/Activity	Number
1806	Troops reviewed by George III on Wanstead Flats	10,000
1804–62	Attending the Easter Hunt. Mounted (on foot)	700–1200 (500–600)
1813–63	People from London at High Beach and Honey Lane Plain	1000s–10,000s
1838–63	Children brought to Epping Forest by van proprietor on an average day (an exceptional day)	1050–1600 (2400)
Pre 1851	Excursionists to High Beach by van weekly before the railway	800–1200
Pre 1851	Excursionists to High Beach by van weekly after the railway	400–600
1863	Industrious classes of London in Forest on Monday mornings	20,000
1863	Visitors in the Forest and at Fairlop Fair	100,000–200,000
1865	Average numbers in Epping Forest on Sundays and Mondays	50,000
1865	Visitors to Epping Forest on Easter Monday by railway and various channels	200,000
1880	Visitors to the Forest on Whit Monday	300,000–400,000
1882	Visitors to Wanstead Flats Fair on Easter Monday	50,000
1882	A Foxhunting Meet	200
1897	Passengers to various stations – Easter Monday	42,864
1897	Passengers to various stations – Whit Monday	51.356
1897	Passengers to various stations – Jubilee Day	37,300
1897	Passengers to various stations – August Bank Holiday	54,396
1914	Bank Holiday visitors to Epping Forest	100,000
1920	Whit Monday arrivals at Chingford Station	100,000
c. 1920	Visitors on Chingford Plain	13,000
c. 1977	Visitors on Chingford Plain	8,000

with resources to travel. In practice, as Buchanan's study shows (Lowe and Goyder, 1983) preservation and opportunism guided the Trust's acquisitions and not considerations of public access or accessibility. However, the inalienable status of land in their ownership did for the greater part secure permanent rights of access at a time when traditional rights of access were being eroded.

For those who enjoyed the new found wealth of a prospering economy of the 1850s and 1860s, the countryside became a place for sport and weekend resort. Country sports, such as fox hunting, deer stalking and grouse and pheasant shooting – traditionally regarded as the sport of kings and the aristocracy, flourished. After the Game Act of 1831 landowners could sell shooting and hunting permits over their land

and once existing owners recognised the value of leasing shooting rights to those with money and the inclination to pay, country sport gained new patronage and new landlords entered the market (Shoard, 1987). At the same time, an educated and cultured few began to regard the countryside as a source of spiritual renewal and inspiration. Reinforcing the eighteenth century landscape taste for the wild and natural landscapes of the uplands, nineteenth century romanticism saw poets, writers and artists alike come to revere and venerate these remote areas. For poets like Wordsworth and Coleridge, the only right and proper way to enjoy the countryside was to walk through these landscapes in solitude and contemplative mood and thereby to achieve a new sense of solace, consciousness and spiritual awareness. Wordsworth denounced 'the crowd' and 'masses' of ordinary society, and he openly opposed the extension of the railway through the Lake District for these reasons. By the end of the nineteenth century, many people came to challenge the materialistic values upon which capitalism, industrialism and city life were founded. The 'freedom to roam' movement which was to gather momentum in the inter-war period was the outward manifestation of many of the same spiritual values Wordsworth and other nineteenth century romantics espoused.

By the 1900s it was clear that not only were people's attitudes to the countryside changing but improvements in public transport and personal mobility meant that the countryside was more accessible to those city residents who had the time and resources to get there. The advent of the bicycle in the 1870s saw recreational cycling quickly established as a leisure time activity and by 1878 the Cyclists' Touring Club had been founded. Motor cycling also quickly established itself as a sport and by 1903 organized races were taking place on public roads around the major cities. The use of the wider countryside for outings and excursions, especially for camping and walking, is reflected in the foundation of the Camping Club of Great Britain and Ireland in 1907. The improvement to personal mobility that the bicycle and motorbike brought meant that some of the demand for recreation which up until then had fallen on urban parks and open spaces was directed to the countryside around the towns and those destinations in the countryside well served by public transport. Much of the popularity of places such as Box Hill and the Surrey Hills and Epping Forest in Essex stems for their location close to railway stations, and the comparative ease with which the Peak District could be reached from the northern cities on foot, bicycle, train and char-a-banc, accounts for its popularity too.

How much of the countryside was accessible and what rights of access people enjoyed once they arrived, depended very much upon local circumstances. The countryside contained a well established network of footpaths and rights of way and for those many people living in the countryside or close to it, habitual use of these tracks was commonplace for getting to work, going to church and to market. However, during the nineteenth century agriculture had undergone a number of changes most notably in respect of new crop patterns, land amalgamation and ownership and in the number of estates which were managed for game as well as sheep. The implications of these changes for those who sought access to the countryside for recreation only became clear during the inter-war period when the freedom to roam movement really gathered momentum (Donnelly, 1986). In addition, a growing demand to engage in a range of informal activities in the countryside as a means of experiencing a new, freer post-war society, was to test the aesthetic and moral sensitivities of landowners and public authorities alike.

The period between the wars

The rise of patriotism that accompanied the Great War and a preoccupation with the benefits of fitness and physical recreation that was left in its wake, had profound repercussions for the way in which recreation demand in Britain was interpreted by central government and local authorities. Concern with the physical condition of urban working-class men had emerged as a matter of political concern at the time of the Boer War (1899–1902) but the aftermath of the First World War meant that national priorities lay with rebuilding the economy and building homes 'fit for heroes' rather than with promoting outdoor recreation.

During the period 1900 to 1939 the area of London quadrupled in size as speculative builders took advantage of the new hinterlands opened up by the extension of rail and underground network and by the proliferation of motor coaches as a rapid means of transport. In London the northern line reached Golders Green in 1907 and opened up the fields of Middlesex for residential development and the metropolitan line followed soon afterwards. South of the Thames, suburban lines were electrified between 1909 and 1932 and suburban sprawl saw the population of Greater London peak at 8.6 million in 1939. Whilst other cities did not show this same spectacular increase, most cities in the Midlands and the north saw the countryside rolling back as suburbia spread (Sheail, 1981). Town planners became increasingly concerned about restraining this outward sprawl as Munton, (1983), Elson, (1986) and Hall et al. (1973) confirm. By 1940 several of the major cities had sketch plans for green belts and while their primary objective was to restrain the outward spread of the urban area, the urban fringe was also regarded as an appropriate location for greater provision of sport and recreational facilities.

Planners came to realise that the urban area could not provide all the open space that was required and they looked to countryside beyond the urban edge to make good any shortfall in provision. In London for example the Minister of Health asked the London County Council (LCC) to survey the need for playing fields and open spaces. Unwin's report presented to the LCC in 1929 identified a shortfall in provision and suggested that the acquisition of land for these purposes should be a priority. His proposal for a girdle of green spaces around London often amounting to no more than 2 km wide was a means of providing recreational facilities but in total would have involved the purchase of some 200 km^2. While the LCC was deliberating over these proposals, other county authorities entered the land market and purchased land for recreational and other purposes. Even so, as Sharp (1984) has shown, the Green Belt failed to live up to recreational expectations. The LCC scheme set the precedent for a much wider public involvement in recreational provision than had been the case to date. But public sector initiatives were challenged repeatedly by shire counties keen to preserve their local environments from the urban hoardes and by those who regarded any form of public intervention in leisure provision as inappropriate.

Many of these early attempts to justify the provision of recreational facilities according to a set of 'open-space standards' were based on estimates of the numbers of youths and adults who would participate in team sports such as football and cricket. This approach reflected a concern to ensure that the next generation of soldiers would be fit to fight in the event of a new war. Team sports such as cricket and football, once a familiar part of village social life and played on street corners throughout the Victorian period, became organised sports through their establishment in state schools and as recreational pursuits promoted by the National Playing Fields Association (NPFA). Formed in 1925 to provide financial assistance for the acquisition of new sports pitches and playing fields, this organization was to set the normative standards of sports provision that were to guide public provision of recreation facilities well into the 1950s (Tourism and Recreation Research Unit, 1983). Progress on acquisition amongst the metropolitan and local authorities was however, slow and piecemeal and much was left to voluntary bodies and private individuals to undertake. Even then the emphasis on organised recreation rather than informal recreation and sports dominated by men, meant that the recreational needs of young children, women, families and the elderly were not addressed and neither were the preferences of those who sought other forms of recreation such as rambling, cycling, riding, and motor sports. As a result, outdoor recreation was interpreted by public authorities as a means of ensuring a fit generation of men and youths rather than a right of citizenship and public provision concentrated almost entirely on improving sports facilities in the urban area. So, although the first tentative steps to place provision for sports and playing fields on a standardised basis were taken during this period and greater involvement of the public sector was sought, progress was slow and selectively addressed the presumed recreational needs of some sections of the public, whilst ignoring others. Other issues arose in the countryside.

Throughout the inter-war period there was a sharp rise in the demand for more informal outdoor pursuits and activities which could be undertaken both on an individual basis and in groups of family and friends. Activities such as rambling, mountaineering, cycling, camping and caravanning all grew in this period and most of this demand fell on the wider countryside. The membership of the Cyclists' Touring Club reached 36,00m by 1939, the Federation of Rambling Clubs founded in 1905, had 40,000 members by 1931 and the Youth Hostels Association (YHA) founded in 1930 had over 83,000 members nine years later. Amongst their followers were a number of socialists with strong patriotic ideals who felt entitled to walk the land they had so recently fought to defend. It was this patriotic fervour, manifest as a natural right to wander at will, that led to head on collisions with other countryside interests – particularly landowners of upland estates who managed the open moor and hill country for game. Such conflicts represented a fundamental clash of attitudes and values that were in part class based but which ultimately reflected differing ideologies of what the countryside and its appropriate enjoyment meant.

Shoard (1987) sees this period as a formative one in the history of countryside conflict whereby proprietorial interests in the countryside allowed landowners to determine where and for what purposes the general public could gain access to the countryside. She sees the involvement of the new prosperous middle-classes in both landownership and countryside sports as the means through which the bourgeoisie came to share those same attitudes to the countryside as the aristocracy. Through the progressive erosion of public rights of access over hill and fell land particularly in the Pennines, extensive areas of the countryside which had been used habitually for walking and rambling were to all intents and purposes 'closed' to the public. Footpaths and roads were ploughed up or closed and the thousands of people who left Sheffield and Manchester to walk the hills at the weekend, found their way barred. To the outcries of local people were added the voices of socialists and welfare organizations and the mass trespasses of the 1930s saw thousands of walkers assert their right to roam freely in the hills.

The trespassers were spurred by a mixture of motives – some deploring the loss of traditional rights which they and their parents had enjoyed; socialists were keen to see a common resource restored to its rightful public, and others like members of the British Workers and Sports Federation had campaigned successfully for football pitches in deprived areas of London and were engaged in organizing open air rambles for young people in the depressed communities of the north. Many were spurred by a mixture of patriotism and a harking back to 'the old beginnings' – sentiments which were especially strong after the war. Others who were politically motivated saw the actions of the landowners as an outward manifestation of capitalism and the freedom of action that the property-owning classes enjoyed at the expense of the working class.

Coming at a time of declining prosperity and job insecurity people looked to the countryside for cheap holidays spent walking, cycling and camping. The phenomenal rise of interest in camping and walking in the countryside that new improved transport facilities brought was also fuelled by the desire of many to relive the communal experiences and excitement of their wartime camping experiences. As Ward and Hardy remark (1986) the First World War was a war fought by conscripts and so guaranteed that the majority of men had experienced camping. With the usual paradox of 'the glow of nostalgia' its veterans remembered the comradeship, the sing-songs and the shared adventures while obliterating the horrors and discomforts of war. Moreover, the superabundance of tents for purchase and the new found mobility conferred by the safety bike, the motor bus and the motor car saw the numbers of people who took to the countryside and coast at weekends and holidays rise consistently throughout the inter-war period. By 1939 some one and a half million people spent their holidays under canvas and in camps of all kinds (Ward and Hardy, 1986).

In this same period the first pioneer holiday camps were founded, often first for men but increasingly for women and children as the Labour movement and local authorities became involved in welfare issues. The prospect of camping, whether in camps or as groups of friends in fields and fell brought the promise of independence, comradeship, and a new kind of social freedom that contrasted with the the dominant values of Victorian society. In this way participation in informal outdoor activities in the countryside became a means of

25

experiencing a new social order that contested established attitudes and values.

Landed interests were quick to respond to the challenge countryside recreation appeared to make to their proprietorial rights. Sheail (1981) records how numerous independent initiatives were taken around the country to try to curb leisure camping and Hardy and Ward (1981) illustrate how similar actions were taken against the expansion of leisure homes on the plotlands of the Thames Valley and the south coast. Early on, attention was focused on safeguarding public health because most camping and building took place in fields or coastal sites without piped water and on sites with inadequate toilet facilities. But other concerns were voiced as well – concerns over bad behaviour, rowdiness and damage to amenity. In Surrey where the heaths and downlands close to London proved attractive to holiday campers,the county council obtained a new clause under its Local Act of 1931 which gave local authorities the right to apply for a court order to close any camp where disruptive behaviour occurred or amenity was harmed. Elsewhere, other local authorities also tried to regulate when and how pleasure camping took place. The Camping Club of Great Britain feared the extension of these local curbs on access to the countryside in general and although by 1935 they had access to about 2,000 sites they anticipated a serious shortage of sites 'if landowners exercised their aesthetic prejudices rather than real evidence of harm to amenity' (Sheail, 1981).

Local Acts at this time exempted some camps from control, for example, military, religious (Salvation Army) and juvenile (Scouts and Guides) camps – acceptable forms of camping where novices would learn the rudiments of good camping. This accolade was soon extended to cover the members and the sites belonging to recognised camping associations. The Home Office however condemned such concessions as discriminating against 'ordinary members of the public who prefer to be independent' although, as Sheail points out, the Camping Club of Great Britain welcomed this recognition when the Public Health Act of 1936 confirmed its exemption from control. Membership then became 'a magic passport to camping freedom and independence'.

This action by local and county authorities also meant that recreational enjoyment of the countryside became institutionalized. Membership of an organization became the accepted means whereby access to land and water could be negotiated with the landowner and 'codes of practice' became the means whereby the organization guaranteed the good behaviour of their membership. In this way the dominant influence of private landed interests in the countryside asserted itself both in the public sector and through their own activities. By determining what kinds of recreational activities were deemed to be acceptable in the countryside, private landed interests became the custodians of 'the countryside aesthetic'. The 'freedom to roam' remained a principle of access championed by the Ramblers' Association but several other recreational interest groups chose to seek permissive and sometimes temporary access to the countryside by organizing themselves and pressing their claims with land owners. As a result, landowners – whether private or public, became the *gatekeepers* to the countryside and the access requirements of people who wished to engage in informal, spontaneous and unorganized recreation were not addressed.

Similar attitudes to recreation also dominated the activities of the Forestry Commission and its involvement in countryside recreation at this time. The Forestry Commission had been created in 1919 in order to secure a national supply of timber but, during the inter-war period, it also became the largest single public authority involved in countryside recreation provision (Sheail, 1981). Its involvement in recreation provision was however, less a response to demand than to a desire to promote an acceptable public image at a time when its activities were being criticized by people seeking recreation in the countryside. A public outcry had accompanied the Commission's coniferous plantations in the Lake District and a prudent Treasury surmised that only by promoting access to the forest estates would more harmonious relations with the public be achieved. By the mid-1930s camping in the Commission's forests had become a popular activity, but lack of suitable water supplies, toilets and overnight accommodation meant that the Camping Club and the YHA argued for improvements in facilities. Coupled with anxieties about damage from forest fires and public health, these concerns saw the Commission arguing in 1935 for their direct involvement in recreation provision in popular sites such as the New Forest and the forests in the west of Scotland. The Treasury eventually accepted this view and in 1936 the first National Forest Park, was opened to the public in Argyllshire. Other Forest Parks followed in the Forest of Dean (1939) and in Snowdonia (1940). Eight Forest Parks had been established by 1955 covering some 7,000 hectares, most of them located in the more remote highland tracts accessible only by car.

The kind of recreation these Parks promoted involved low-key pursuits such as walking, rambling, nature study and some sailing and fishing. Camping was regulated by permit and restricted to specific time periods in the year but these restrictions did not prevent thousands of visitors from enjoying these forest environments. The first

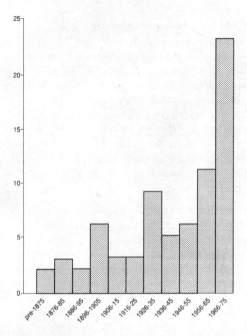

Figure 2.1: Dates of formation of national environmental groups 1875–1975
Source: Lowe & Goyder, 1983

major involvement of public agencies in countryside recreation provision proved to be a popular one and set the scene for wider state involvement in recreation provision after the second world war. However, the kind of recreation deemed to be acceptable in Forest Parks – regulated, quiet, and disciplined – appealed to some people rather than others *and* was a means of deflecting public concern from their wider reafforestation activities in areas over which the public had previously enjoyed permissive access.

In the light of these early experiences it is not surprising to find that the number of organizations concerned with outdoor activities and environmental protection and enjoyment also grew during the interwar years (Figure 2.1). The British Field Sports Society founded in 1930 included angling, fishing and hunting and falconry amongst its activities; associations for gliding and flying were formed and flourished immediately after the war and the British Canoe Union was founded in 1936. Significant too, were the formation of Angling Associations and the Rambler's Association in 1935 which included a strong working class element among their membership. Membership of other organizations concerned with camping, orienteering and walking, such as the YHA and camping clubs also continued to grow. The organization which perhaps best represents the overall concern for environmental protection that had prompted numerous ad hoc initiatives to protect archeological sites, sites of particular beauty and natural history interest, was the Council for the Preservation of Rural England (CPRE) founded in 1926.

First proposed by Abercrombie who had played an instrumental role in promoting planning as a means of regulating where development took place around expanding towns and cities, the CPRE sought 'to organize concerted action to secure the protection of rural scenery and the amenities of country towns and villages from 'disfigurement or injury'. It aimed to provide advice about how to achieve these objectives as well. These essentially preservationist objectives were coupled with Abercrombie's vision of planning as both an instrument of control and of promotion (Abercrombie, 1945). He saw planning as a means of securing harmonious development – the essential qualities of the countryside could be retained by regulating growth and promoting its 'rational' enjoyment. Underlying the whole was a concern to ensure that housing design and lay out were integrated with the provision of adequate services such as roads and open spaces. Critical to his vision and that of CPRE was the concept of 'rational enjoyment of the countryside' in which some forms of recreational activity would be regarded as acceptable and other clearly not. Only certain kinds of camps were acceptable, only certain kinds of leisure homes were acceptable and only certain kinds traditional rather than modern sports were acceptable. 'Considerate recreational use of the countryside' became the phrase of the day – a phrase to be enshrined later in the National Parks legislation of 1949.

Underlying this concept was the growing fear that the recreational tastes of a newly prosperous working class conflicted with those who, until that date, had been the main beneficiaries of the recreational opportunities of the countryside – the landowners (Bennett et al. 1986). Not only did urban workers seem to enjoy themselves in new and different ways but changing transport facilities and leisure time provided them with many more opportunities to take to the countryside in large numbers and to new destinations. Popular recreation had become a threat to the aesthetic and moral sensitivities of country landowners including local authorities and ultimately to their ability to control where, when and how, people enjoyed the countryside. Throughout this period public intervention and the activities of several voluntary groups concerned with environmental protection promoted rational enjoyment of the countryside as the most appropriate way of enjoying it – that is the quiet, contemplative appreciation of wild landscapes. In pursuit of this ideology, this same alliance joined forces with private landowners to contain where and how other more active and socially motivated enjoyment of the wider countryside took place. The need to preserve the countryside became all important and as Sheail remarks, many of the concepts and policies which were to guide rural planning in the post-war period were already in place when the war broke out.

The inter-war years had seen the first of many conflicts in the countryside that stemmed from people's differing expectations about what form countryside recreation should take and where it could take place. A preoccupation with the need to ensure a fit and healthy nation had guided the limited intervention made by municipal authorities in sports provision and much of this was confined to the urban area. However, the popular appeal of other forms of informal recreation such as camping, walking and motor sports had prompted some local authorities to purchase common land as public open-space only to regulate its use by the imposition of local by-laws. As a result popular forms of outdoor enjoyment were regulated both by the public sector and through organizations which themselves were required to operate codes of conduct before they could gain access to rural land. Many outdoor activities became organized in this way and membership became the means of gaining access to the countryside environments people sought. Unorganized and informal enjoyment of the countryside whether for outdoor sports, camping, strolling or motoring in the countryside was not provided for by these actions. Moreover, whereas much of the recreational demand had previously fallen on land in and around the towns and cities, mass participation in countryside recreation meant that increasingly demand was to fall on the wider countryside where the inviolability of property rights meant that landowners maintained their dominant influence as custodians of the countryside aesthetic. National Parks were seen as one means of both protecting those landscapes the idealists of the inter-war period had come to cherish most and of enabling more people to enjoy them safe in the knowledge that anyone could wander over them at will. The events of the immediate post-war period were to see these expectations thwarted when what had been championed as 'the people's charter for open air' became emasculated by parliament and the reassertion of landowners' property rights (Shoard, 1987, Blunden and Curry, 1989).

The post-war period up to 1960

Gordon Cherry in his official history of environmental planning, (Cherry, 1975) describes how the 'demand for a better Britain' which dominated the immediate post-war period, exerted pressure on successive governments to demonstrate that the state could provide real improvements in the quality of life so many had earned. The National Parks and Access to the Countryside Act of 1949 and the Town and Country Planning Act of 1947 were both designed to provide some of the improvements people wanted. The latter introduced new development control powers which were invested with local and county authorities. Development plans guided changes in land-use and post-war reconstruction programmes set about trying to provide a comprehensive approach to residential and industrial development in which the best of both the town and the countryside were to be promoted. Improvements in amenity and open-space provision were both embraced in these programmes. In the urban area slum clearance schemes provided the opportunity to incorporate open-spaces where they were most needed although in practice few new parks or open spaces were provided. Burgess Park in London was one of the few new open spaces added to the inner city areas in this way (TRRU, 1983). In the countryside around towns private individuals, voluntary organizations and the National Trust continued to secure land for the public's enjoyment on an ad hoc and opportunist basis. But many planners continued to advocate a much more prominent role for public authorities in the provision of recreational facilities and open space. It is in this period too that national Green Belt legislation was passed (Ministry of Housing and Local Government, 1955). As a result recreational use of land on the edge of cities became regarded as consistent with maintaining the open landscape of green belts but was never accepted as a reason for establishing them (Munton, 1983, Elson, 1986).

In the spirit of optimism which accompanied the post-war reconstruction programme, Abercrombie's Plan for the London County Council of 1945 for example, recognized the need to plan for a comprehensive range of open space facilities that anticipated increasing demand for both formal and informal recreation. It sought to provide attractive environments in which people could work and play. His proposal for a green chain around London, served the purpose of not only providing for a variety of outdoor pursuits but also provided a means of linking the city with the countryside so that all sections of the population could benefit. The pattern of open spaces he proposed included provision for children's playgrounds, town squares and amenity spaces, school playing fields, landscaped town parks, large playing fields for adults and senior children, recreation and sports centres, connecting and radiating parkways, wedges of open land, small green belts and strips of open space for defining the boundaries of communities, commons and heathlands, river embankments, green belt reservations, areas of high scenic value and normal farmland.

That the local authorities failed to respond to this imaginative and far sighted proposal is not surprising given their limited ability to fund and acquire land for these purposes. Although the LCC had acquired a limited number of properties for use by the public for recreation under the 1938 Green Belt Act, progress had been slow and piecemeal and the post-war development plans provided little guidance about how and where recreational provision should be made or about what priorities should be pursued. Rather than recognizing the multiplicity of recreational needs championed by Abercrombie in his plans, public authorities often adopted a 'standards' approach to provision that was a legacy of the inter-war period with its heavy emphasis on organised sport rather than on a wider range of individual and family pursuits. Moreover, whilst these standards were based on the number of active members of the population who might be expected to participate in team sports and organised games and the number of sports pitches and playing fields these participants suggested, even the minimum standard of provision of 2.4 hectares (6 acres) per 1000 head of population could not be met in the inner cities. These inner areas had little chance of fulfilling the NPFA standard of 4 hectares (10 acres) per 1000 population recommended by the Ministry of Town and Country Planning in 1945. By 1950 the LCC had reduced the level of provision to 1 hectare per thousand (LCC, 1950) partly in recognition of the impossibility of meeting even the minimum standards in the built up area and partly in the belief that provision in a green belt could make good any deficiencies encountered in the urban area itself. Implicit in such a judgement is that provision beyond the urban area is accessible to those who have most need – those in the inner city, and that the type of facilities envisaged (sports pitches) is itself what people want.

In the absence of any attempts to discover what kinds of facilities and environments people preferred or were most in need of, this normative approach to open-space planning prevailed amongst most urban authorities well into the 1960s (Veal, 1987). Significant for the role that the urban-fringe would come to play in recreational policies pursued by the Countryside Commission and local authorities in the late 1960s, is the fact that the recreational role of the countryside around cities was used both to justify the implementation of green belts and as an excuse for lowering the standards of recreational provision of those inner city communities most in need of improved amenities and recreational facilities. For as Ward and Hardy's study (1986) shows it was the newly emerging white-collar workers and not workers on the factory floor who benefited from improvements in holiday entitlement and from the new forms of holiday opportunities offered by the second generation of commercialized holiday camps which burgeoned during this period. Car-owners too were drawn from the better-off workers and whilst the number of people who spent a holiday away from home rose from 15 million to 30 million in the period 1937–1949, for the lower paid workers, holidays away from the city were still the exception rather than the rule. Many poorly paid workers continued to live out their lives in areas where open space provision was below standards advocated by national bodies like the Central Council for Physical Recreation and where even the provision of school sport facilities – mandatory after the Education Act of 1945, did little to extend provision to the wider community or outside the school years. In this respect the experience of London was typical of other major cities.

Elson for example details the history of the post-war green belt plans and shows how a desire to retain attractive landscape close to where most people lived, coupled with a desire to preserve recreational land, nominally accessible to needy sections of the population, guided these early proposals rather than detailed appraisals of who needed recreational facilities and which areas were in most need of improvements in supply. However, by 1957, when the Local Government Circular 50/57 set out the objectives for permanent green belts, recreational needs on their own could not be used to justify designation. Instead the circular stated that green belts could only be established in order to:

* check the further growth of a large built-up area;

* prevent neighbouring towns from merging into one another;

* preserve the special character of a town.

By placing greater emphasis on restraint and the preservation of open land rather than on particular land-use outcomes, the circular set the guidelines within which all subsequent planning applications in the green belts were to be judged for the next 25 years, including those which related to recreational provision such as golf courses, country clubs, safari parks, riding stables, motor circuits, caravan parks and camping sites. Overall therefore, although the planners and social reformers continued to advocate a more active and prominent role for state intervention in recreation provision, any improvements in provision continued to be based on the 'standards' and values which

33

had guided provision in the inter- war years. Moreover, the limited intervention of public authorities in the land market at this time meant that the voluntary sector and charitable trusts retained a prominent role and their activities were guided by ad hoc land purchase rather than by a policy of acquisition informed by the expressed needs of their membership or the general public. Over the period as a whole therefore, although green belts were designated, any improvements in recreation provision were incidental and a by-product of restraint rather than positive actions based on an informed understanding of recreational needs.

In the wider countryside the National Parks and Access to the Countryside Act of 1949 addressed provision for public enjoyment of the countryside of a rather different kind to that which urban fringe locations could provide. The Act marked the culmination of a long struggle to preserve and retain access to some of the most outstanding areas in England and Wales in which the numerous recreational and amenity groups founded during the inter-war period played a prominent part (Blunden and Curry, 1989). From the outset, the twin objectives of the Act meant that it was likely to prove inherently difficult to implement, but as several commentators point out, (MacEwen and MacEwen, 1981 and Newby, 1979), the Act was based upon a number of false assumptions about access, recreation and preservation.

The Act established the National Parks Commission with powers to designate National Parks and it charged the Commission with not only preserving and enhancing the natural beauty of the parks' landscapes, but also with providing opportunities for outdoor recreation within them. The parks were to be administered by Boards or Committees of county councils with a third of their membership contributed by government appointees. Without appropriate powers and funds to purchase land for these purposes however, and without an appropriate organizational structure with which to influence decisions of the local authorities who were to administer them, the parks failed to live up to the expectations many people had invested in them. As in the countryside at large, the main ways in which harmonious development in the parks was to be ensured was through the development control system rather than through national ownership of land and private landownership continued to dominate within the parks (Figure 2.2). Moreover, it was assumed that farmers, acting as good husbanders of resources, would ensure the continued preservation of the outstanding landscapes the parks sought to protect.

With the benefit of hindsight we now know that both these assumptions were ill-founded. As the MacEwens demonstrate, all kinds of developments have taken place in the National Parks since their

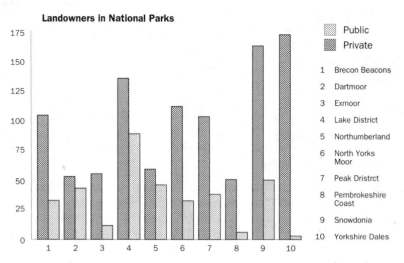

Landowners in National Parks

Legend:
- Public
- Private

1   Brecon Beacons
2   Dartmoor
3   Exmoor
4   Lake District
5   Northumberland
6   North Yorks Moor
7   Peak Dristrct
8   Pembrokeshire Coast
9   Snowdonia
10   Yorkshire Dales

Figure 2.2: Landownership in National Parks
Source: MacEwen & MacEwen, 1981

designation while Blacksell and Gilg (1981) and others (Anderson, 1981 and Countryside Commission 1989c) have pointed to the inability of development control to significantly affect the rate and type of landscape change in the National Parks and the Areas of Outstanding Natural Beauty (AONBs) the Act also identified. In addition, a prosperous post-war agriculture which pursued increased yields and efficiency coupled with the accelerated rate at which the Forestry Commission extended its planting activities, meant that these landscapes changed apace. Agriculture and forestry continued to be regarded as benign rural activities but they neither conserved the arcadian landscape of a traditional farm economy so many country lovers recalled, nor sustained the viable rural communities so many hankered after. Critically too, the Act was predicated on the assumption that the kind of recreation the freedom to roam movement had been based upon would continue to be the dominant recreational activity in these area. It assumed that the values of solitude, spiritual renewal and physical prowess this movement cherished most, reflected commonly-held values and that people would be primarily motivated to visit the National Parks for these same reasons. An assumption that 'mass, car-based countryside recreation' was to test severely.

Given these assumptions it is not so surprising to find that the National Parks were designated primarily to protect the outstanding and often geographically remote landscapes of the uplands while

35

other lowland areas were accorded the lesser status of Areas of Out-standing Natural Beauty (AONB). True to the aspirations of the free-dom to roam movement, emphasis in the Act was placed on securing access on foot through the parks in particular and over the countryside in general. It did this in two ways. First, local planning authorities could enter into Access Agreements with landowners whereby the landowner agreed to allow public access over a given area for a period of years, in return for grants and assistance with wardening. Second, it made all local authorities responsible for preparing and reviewing rights-of-way maps and thereby determined to prevent any further erosion of public rights of access.

The Act did much to halt the loss of public rights of way that had taken place in the Peak District for example but, in practice, the Act provid-ed that the public should have 'no right of access to open country whether in a National Park or not, except by agreement or order.' (MacEwen and MacEwen, 1981 p.19). In these respects the Act left the proprietorial rights of landowners largely unaltered and did little to promote a new set of land values which might better reflect the inter-ests of a wider public. With the benefit of hindsight too, we find that access agreements have been little used. Gibbs and Whitby (1975) show that 80% of the area covered by the some 98 access areas estab-lished under this provision lie in the National Parks and 56% lies in the Peak. In the wider countryside only Surrey and Hampshire in the south-east and Staffordshire and Lancashire in the north-west have used these agreements. They proved costly to implement and difficult to negotiate and while the Act broke new ground in giving the public statutory rights over recognized footpaths, bridleways and roads used as public paths, many counties did not keep the situation under review and numerous Rights of Way were not maintained. In a period of national reconstruction when road building rather than pedestrian access took precedence, it is not surprising to find that the highway authorities, with whom the responsibilities for Rights of Way lay, failed to take their responsibilities seriously. Twenty five years after this legislation first entered the statute books, a national survey (Countryside Commission, 1990) demonstrated that highway author-ities were still failing to carry out their responsibilities (Figure 2.3).

At a time when more and more people were coming to enjoy visiting the countryside as an extension of social life and in ways that were symbolic of a new society in which social interaction and shared enjoyment rather than just spiritual renewal, self-awareness and physical fitness found popular appeal, the values which underpinned the National Parks Act seemed curiously out of tune with the mood of the nation as a whole. The outstanding landscapes protected by the

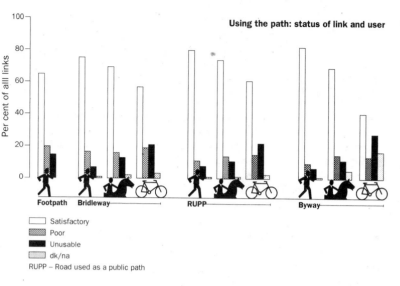

Figure 2.3: Conditions of the Rights of Way network
Source: Countryside Commission, 1990

Act were remote from most centres of population and the 'considerate use' of these areas the Act identified, favoured quiet, solitary and aesthetic appreciation of wild landscapes rather than more diverse, active and gregarious forms of enjoyment. And in the same way that the Act enshrined certain sets of values and not others, it also precipitated a fundamental division between recreationists and nature conservationists – a division which was to be reversed in 1991 with the dismembering of the Nature Conservancy Council.

In the same year that the National Parks Act was established, the government set up the Nature Conservancy (later the Nature Conservancy Council [NCC]) with responsibility for establishing and managing nature reserves and providing advice on nature conservation. For John Dower who had been one of the main architects of the National Parks legislation, this division of responsibilities cut through one of his central tenets. He believed passionately that nature should neither be divorced from landscape nor from people's enjoyment of the natural world around them – national parks and nature conservation should be in the same hands. But the government of the day accepted the advice of scientists who argued strongly that it was not possible to manage reserves without scientific advice which itself needed to be based on research. In their view no National Park Authority was likely to contain the kind of expert advice needed to carry out these dual activities. Accordingly, the NC was given powers to enter into agreements with landowners for the management of nature reserves, to buy land for this purpose – compulsorily if required – and to make by-laws for their protection. It was also empowered to carry out research.

The implications of this division for visitors to the countryside was that nature reserves were excluded from access agreements and became scientific laboratories rather than places for the public to enjoy. Sheail (1988) shows that even in the 1950s local people viewed the activities of the Conservancy with real concern. In Scotland for example,the absence of National Parks meant that there was no authority to champion the cause of access and when the Conservancy proposed to establish a reserve of some 15,000 hectares in the Cairngorms, local people feared least the proposed reserve bring by-laws which would make 'all our youngsters trespassers in the land of our birth and threaten visitors with fines and and penalties.' (Sheail, 1988, p.5).

Against this background, the decision by members of the Conservancy to emphasise its scientific basis rather than the wider benefits to society that might be gained from experiencing nature first hand, ensured that nature conservation became accepted as ideologically neutral and value free. In this way, Lowe and Goyder suggest (1981) that the cause of nature conservation, which was to spawn numerous voluntary organizations in the 1950s, avoided controversy. But their motives for doing so, as others have remarked (Cox, 1988 and Green, 1981) often had more in common with the private landed interests rather than with those of organizations which championed the wider appreciation of the natural world and its essential role in contributing to a better quality of life, like the Ramblers' Association (Mabey, 1980).

Conclusion

The attitudes and values enshrined in the National Parks Act epitomise the ideology of the countryside aesthetic and were to guide public sector involvement in countryside recreation throughout much of the post-war period. Similarly, the appropriation of nature by the scientific community instituted by the formation of the Nature Conservancy heralded a period in post-war land-use planning that favoured science as a value-free and neutral arbiter of conflicting demands on the countryside. As long as the austerity of the immediate post-war period prevented most people from taking to the countryside on a regular basis and from pursuing new forms of recreational activities, conflicts between people seeking different ways of enjoying the countryside and between visitors and nature conservationists were subdued. All the parks, save the Peak District National Park, were located at some distance from the main centres of demand, and were only accessible on a regular basis by car. The nearest park to the South-East – the fastest growing region in post-war Britain, was the Brecon Beacons National Park and that was four to five hours away. But, by the end of the 1950s most people were beginning to share in the rising prosperity of a expanding economy and car ownership became the norm rather than the exception. Then, the parks and the countryside as a whole came under new kinds of recreational pressure for which they were unprepared. By the 1960s, it was clear that a new leisured society had arrived and with it a new set of recreational demands and environmental conflicts. But outside the National Parks, the pattern of sites acquired as Public Open Spaces by local authorities and voluntary organizations provided a legacy of provision which subsequent initiatives taken by the public sector did little to alter. Moreover, the prevailing ideology of countryside recreation as the quiet contemplative appreciation of wild scenery, ensured that new recreation activities and new aspirations and expectations generated by a prosperous post-war society would prove difficult to accommodate in a countryside still dominated by private, landed interests – unless the public sector chose to pursue them directly.

3

Trends and issues in countryside recreation: 1960 to Recreation 2000

....

Introduction

Throughout the 1960s and early 1970s outdoor recreation continued to grow at a spectacular rate (Countryside Commission, 1980a). The number of visitors recorded out in the countryside on summer weekends increased almost exponentially as did participation in outdoor sports (Figure 3.1). Patmore and Rogers (1973) for example, estimate that some 9 million day trips would have been generated on a summer week end in 1968, and by 1977 when the first National Survey of Countryside Recreation was completed this figure had doubled (Fitton, 1979). In the London region alone the percentage of adults who made a visit to the countryside on a summer Sunday rose from 7% in 1964 to 20% in 1972 with the percentage amongst adult car-owners rising to almost double this figure. On a regional scale this level of demand suggested that some one and a half million people made trips into the countryside around London at a weekend and in the North West an average of 26 trips per 100 people were made during a summer week in the mid-sixties (Patmore and Rogers, 1973). Traffic in the Lake District National Park doubled in the decade after the Park was designated in 1951 and increased by over half again in the the following decade. Such evidence did indeed suggest that Dower's 'Fourth Wave' was breaking across the countryside (Dower, 1965).

The trends in outdoor sports over this same period illustrate a similar pattern. The Sports Council estimates that by 1981 total participation in sport had increased by 150% since 1960 and both the number and types of people participating and the diversity of activities pursued had increased (Sports Council, 1983). For example outdoor sports such as water skiing, motors sports and cycling showed high growth

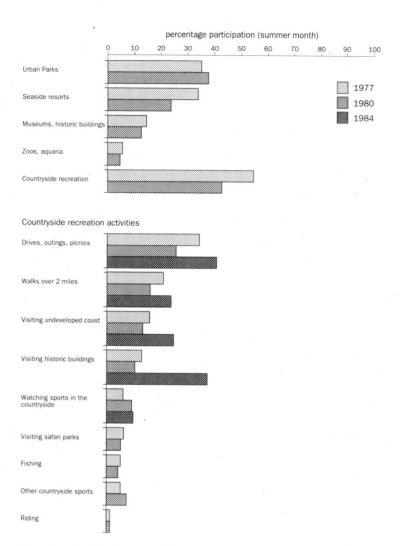

Figure 3.1: Participation in outdoor recreation activities 1977–1984
Source: Countryside Commission, 1982 and 1985a

rates. Membership of water ski clubs rose from 3280 in 1965 to over 10000 in 1980 and in the same period the number of competitors licensed by the RAC for motor sports grew from 19,000 to 30,500 (Sports Council, 1983). By the early 1980s, six of the ten largest outdoor sports organizations were those whose activities took place for

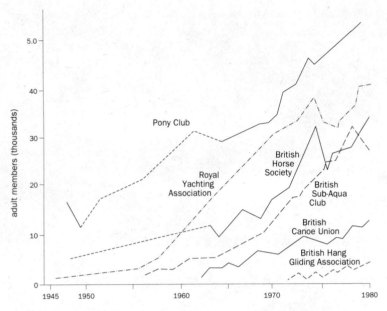

Figure 3.2: Participation in selected outdoor sports 1945–1980
Source: Sports Council, 1983

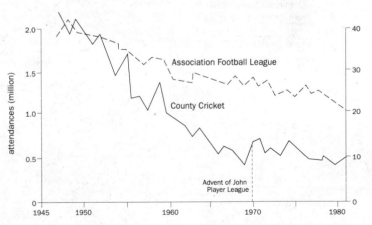

Figure 3.3: Trends in Spectator Sports 1945–1980
Source: Sports Council, 1983

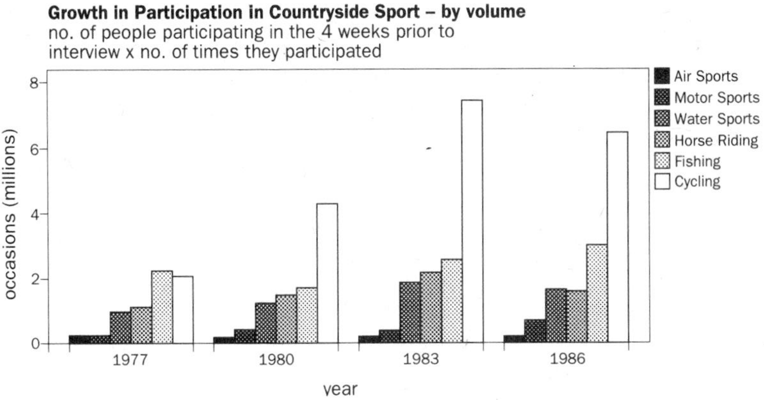

Growth in Participation in Countryside Sport – by volume
no. of people participating in the 4 weeks prior to
interview x no. of times they participated

Figure 3.4: Growth in participation in Countryside Sport by volume
Source: Sports Council, 1990

the greater part in the countryside – three Golf unions, the National Federation of Anglers and the Camping and Caravanning Club (Sports Council 1986). Only spectator sports such as football and horse racing showed declining participation during this same period (Figures 3.2, 3.3, 3.4).

Dower attributed the rapid growth in demand to rising affluence of society as a whole, to the increased leisure time most people enjoyed and critically to the increase in personal mobility mass car-ownership brought. With a seemingly limitless increase in the demand for outdoor recreation and a limited supply of open countryside deliberately set aside for recreation, it is easy to understand why in the 1960s and 70s leisure planners and managers regarded this phenomenal growth in demand as something of a challenge. All the more so, when to these concerns were added the voices of environmentalists intent on demonstrating the environmental limits to growth and the need to conserve natural resources – especially the countryside and wild areas mass recreation seemed destined to destroy. At the national level however, the newly elected Labour government of 1964 saw the rising tide of leisure as an opportunity for all people to enjoy a better life and, as part of its broad programme of social reform, it set about determining and encouraging a national recreation strategy. 'Planning for leisure' became the key phrase of the period as the public sector was encouraged to pursue socially motivated policies of 'Sport for All' and 'Countryside Recreation for All' (Coalter et al., 1986). The often equivocal and sometimes hostile response these policies drew from

43

local authorities which were the primary providers of facilities during this period was influenced by several factors.

First, outdoor recreation as a set of activities was institutionally divided into those which were primarily regarded as sports – the responsibility of the Advisory Sports Council 1965 and later in 1971 the Sports Council (SC), and countryside recreation which became the responsibility of a newly constituted body within the Department of the Environment – the Countryside Commission in 1968. In practice this institutional separation meant that provision of outdoor recreation in the urban area was invested with the local authorities because the SC came to focus its attention on organized sports requiring substantial investment in facilities. Countryside recreation by definition took place outside the urban area and the Countryside Commission's remit was accordingly restricted by arbitrary administrative boundaries. In functional terms this division also meant the Countryside Commission could only influence demand indirectly by altering supply because it was forced to operate outside the urban area. The main way in which the Commission came to influence demand outside the National Parks was through a spatial policy of provision focused on particular sites in the urban fringe.

Second, at the same time that demand for outdoor recreation was expanding apace, the modern environmental movement was also gaining momentum (Lowe and Goyder, 1983). As these authors point out, the late 1950s and the mid-1970s were both periods of sudden growth of new environmental groups when more people came to 'count the mounting external costs of unbridled economic growth and sought to reassert non-material values' (p.25). Mass participation in countryside recreation by car-borne visitors was just one manifestation of non-material values but as a result countryside recreation became regarded as an environmental threat alongside other external costs of economic growth like pollution, pesticides and nuclear weapons. Amongst the shire counties which were the recipients of a huge increase in visitors, recreation became an activity to be controlled rather than encouraged. In consequence, this period saw a growing rift between the promotional policies advocated by central government and its agencies on the one hand and the protectionist attitudes of environmental groups with a strong rural base and the local authorities in the rural counties responsible for providing facilities and infra-structure, on the other.

Third, both central and local government exhibited an unswerving belief in the ability of planning to provide optimum solutions to the problem of leisure demand and environmental protection. Regional and Structure Planning were both prominent activities which planners engaged in during the 1960s and early 1970s. As a result, surveys of leisure demand, patterns of activity and countryside resources were undertaken often on a regional basis. But, consistent with protecting proprietorial rights of rural landowners, central government never identified recreation as a key issue for formal consideration in structure plans, preferring instead to regard leisure provision in the countryside as a discretionary activity. This prevailing view meant that attempts by the Countryside Commission and the Regional Councils for Sport and Recreation to co-ordinate a national recreation policy informed by the findings of these regional and local surveys was constantly frustrated by the lack of support amongst the shire authorities. As Coalter shows (Coalter et al., 1986), by the late 1970s the Countryside Commission had progressively withdrawn from its involvement with structure planning and instead came to concentrate its activities on demonstrating how improvements in countryside recreation facilities and landscape could be achieved 'outside the planning system' through area management experiments.

Fourth, by the mid-1970s local authorities were operating under new financial constraints precipitated by the oil-crisis of 1973 and a world recession. Financial cuts and an absence of consensus amongst planners about the kind of future they were planning for, meant that local authorities came to review their spending priorities. In an area of discretionary expenditure such as leisure services, public authorities turned increasingly to the voluntary sector and to self-help approaches to achieve cost-effective forms of recreation provision and landscape improvement (Countryside Recreation Research Advisory Group, 1979). Such an approach was to find increasing favour at the national level too. With the return in 1979 of a Conservative government dedicated to the pursuit of market-economics in every sector of economic life, public leisure services like all other social services became subject to a new set of economic strictures.

Lastly, even before the return of a Conservative government in 1979, there were signs that the 'Fourth Wave' had begun to abate and demand for countryside recreation was not growing exponentially. Successive national recreation surveys conducted during the 1980s revealed that demand for countryside recreation had levelled off but changes within the range of recreational activities seeking access to the countryside meant that both new problems and opportunities needed addressing. The purpose of this chapter is to explore how each of these separate strands of institutional, political, social and attitudinal change impinged on the kind of public policies pursued for countryside recreation. It concludes by identifying a range of issues which emerged at the time of the Countryside Commission's major review of countryside recreation policy undertaken during 1985–7 and called *Recreation 2000* (Countryside Commission, 1985).

The institutionalization of outdoor recreation

Interestingly, in the light of the emphasis nature conservationists had placed on the scientific justification for their activities in the immediate post-war period, so too Michael Dower chose to present the threat posed by the fourth wave in terms of a biological and seemingly 'value-free' analogy – carrying capacity (Dower, 1965). He argued that only by matching recreational demand with a suitable supply of recreational resources would the destruction of the countryside be halted and, like Abercrombie before, he advocated a spatial approach to provision based on the recreational carrying capacity of the city and its city-region. For Dower, the increase in countryside recreation was just one manifestation of an increase in the demand for leisure which would embrace a whole range of activities and environmental settings both in the urban areas and the surrounding countryside. The institutional organization of outdoor recreation alighted on by the Government did little justice to this vision.

Unlike Dower's vision of an integrated approach to provision in which the city and its region were to have formed the basic planning unit, institutional provision separated leisure provision and planning both functionally and geographically. The Advisory Sports Council (ASC) established in 1965 had responsibilities for advising government on matters relating to 'the development of amateur sport and physical recreation, to foster co-operation among statutory authorities and voluntary organizations and to establish priorities for expenditure.' The central role of provision was to be played by the local authorities but the ASC through its research orientation and studies of demand for sport, exhorted local authorities to increase provision using the twin principles of 'standards of provision' and 'maximum utilization of resources' as the basis for determining deficiency and expanding opportunities. These principles are clearly related to the normative approach to sports provision which had been applied in the urban area since the 1940s and reflect a requirement to better co-ordinate provision at a time when the rising affluence of all sections of society was expected to be translated directly into an exponential demand for facilities.

The establishment of the Countryside Commission, with the responsibility for preserving and enhancing the natural beauty and amenity of the countryside and securing and improving public access to it for purposes of open air recreation, followed the recommendations of the 1966 White Paper, *Leisure in the Countryside* (Ministry of Land and Natural Resources, 1966). The main thrust of this paper had been to focus on the resolution of what by this time had come to be regarded as the main problem namely: how to balance the needs of those who lived and worked in the country with the needs of visitors? At the institutional level the Countryside Commission for England and Wales was given responsibilities for resolving these problems in the countryside as a whole and not just within the areas of the National Parks. The primary way in which the Commission sought to address this problem was through grant-aid to local authorities and through disseminating the results of their research and experimentation functions which they also acquired. Even so, how the Countryside Commission came to execute their responsibilities owes much to the reasoning employed in the White Paper itself and the assumptions it was based on.

The White Paper identified several concerns. First, not only was there mounting concern at the growing numbers of people who currently visited the countryside but, there was also an expectation that these numbers would continue to grow at an accelerating rate. Second, landowners were concerned least the continued growth of motorized recreation would bring people who were untutored in the ways of the countryside into conflict with farmers and their farming operations. Problems such as trespass, vandalism and loss of farm income seemed to be an inevitable outcome if an exponential increase in visitors were to be allowed to spill over into the wider countryside. Third, there was increasing concern amongst environmentalists that the capacity of certain popular sites in the countryside to sustain increasing numbers of visitors was limited and wildlife and physical resources would be damaged as a result. And to the voice of conservationists were added those other groups like CPRE who feared that the very essence of countryside enjoyment would itself be lost as more and more people sought out the countryside.

The White Paper alludes frequently to the need to control and restrain where demand fell in the countryside. It also expresses a belief that many new participants in countryside recreation seemed to enjoy the countryside by having little more than somewhere to park their car and the company of others of like mind. The solution to these anticipated problems and the assumed predilictions of the majority of visitors was an emphasis on measures to *contain* where people went in the countryside. It was argued that by creating new facilities in the countryside close to where demand lay, visitors would be attracted to them and as a result some of the pressure would be taken off the

National Parks and the farmed countryside. The Country Park, Picnic Site and to a lesser extent the Regional Park, became the main instruments through which the Commission implemented this policy of constraint and opportunity and the urban fringe was identified as the most appropriate place for locating them.

In the words of the White Paper country parks were to serve three purposes:

> 'They would make it easier for town-dwellers to enjoy their leisure in the open, without travelling too far and adding to the congestion on the roads; they would ease the pressure in the more remote and solitary places; and they would reduce the risk of damage to the countryside – aesthetic as well as physical – which often comes about when people merely settle down for an hour or a day where it suits them, somewhere 'in the country' – to the inconvenience and indeed expense of the countryman who lives there.'

The assumptions upon which this 'deflector' role for Country Parks are based are several and are more fully explored in Chapter 4, suffice it to say at this point that they include assumptions about the motivations, attitudes and values that underpin demand for countryside recreation and about the ability of Country Parks to provide the range of pleasures and environments people seek when out in the countryside. This unitary response to the spectre of the Fourth Wave was a pale shadow of Dower's vision of a comprehensive range of recreational facilities and environmental settings.

The rise of environmentalism

At the same time that central government came to interpret the growth in demand for countryside recreation as both an opportunity for more people to enjoy a better quality of life and a potential threat to the productive interests in the countryside, other environmental groups were pointing to the potential threat economic growth itself posed to the future of the natural environment and society as a whole (Lowe and Goyder, 1983). Pepper's (1984) discussion of the roots of modern environmentalism shows that while some of those same spiritual values which had fired the nineteenth century romantics and the patriotic and nostalgic concerns of the freedom to roam movement of the interwar period continued to be reflected in post-war environmentalism, new beliefs about how 'progress' was to be achieved, were also added to them. For example, in the series of meetings held in the the 1960s called the 'Countryside in 1970' conferences (Council for Nature, 1966) concern was expressed not only about the obvious threats to the countryside such as development and recreation but also about the insidious threats which agricultural pesticides, industrial pollution and economic growth itself posed to the survival of wildlife and to society as a whole (Moore, 1987, Sheail, 1985). In this way environmentalism in the 1970s evolved into a complex and multi-faceted movement which embraced a wide range of issues and values.

Even though complex, Pepper points out that two main lines of thought or belief systems characterize these new environmentalists. The one based on 'ecocentric' beliefs and the other on 'technocentric' beliefs. His analysis of these two central belief helps to explain the attitudes and actions of several environmental groups and public authorities towards countryside recreation in the 1970s and 1980s. The beliefs and values of 'ecocentric' environmentalism lie closely with those of nineteenth century romanticism and place human beings firmly within nature. Because the individual is a part of nature, 'for his (sic) own sake he should not plunder, exploit and destroy natural ecosystems – because in doing so he is destroying the biological foundation of his own life.' (Pepper, 1986, p.28). Seen in this light social systems like any other natural system are governed by natural laws and a limit on economic growth as well as a fundamental change in attitudes and values is required if 'progress' in forging a new relationship between nature and society is to be achieved.

Few environmental groups concerned with the countryside per se adhere to these ecocentric values although the Friends of the Earth probably approximate closest to them (Lowe and Goyder, 1983). Rather, most environmental groups follow Hardin's approach to the 'problem of the commons' and advocate enlightened private ownership as the best means of guarding the countryside. Many such groups justify their actions as a means of ensuring the rights of nature itself and of benefiting the future of mankind. Amongst groups with an interest in outdoor recreation only the Ramblers' Association can be said to pursue a truly enlightened approach with its belief in the principle of de facto access to the countryside as the only means of ensuring that everyone can enjoy the countryside. Other environmental groups such as the Royal Society for the Protection of Birds (RSPB), The Woodland Trust and the Wildfowl and Wetlands Trust and outdoor activity groups such as anglers, mountaineers and motor sports organizations, seek to acquire land for their own purposes or enter into sole access agreements with land-owners (Centre for Leisure Research, 1984). In reaching these agreements other users are effectively excluded. This tendency to treat the countryside as a positional good rather than a common property resource, has been apparent throughout the history of countryside recreation, but as Chapter 4 will show, it has become an increasing tendency in recent years. As a result, although many environmentalists espouse ecocentric beliefs, the mechanism they favour for ensuring the rights of nature and the future of mankind are firmly based on proprietorial rights and the operation of free-market forces.

Contrasted with the beliefs of ecocentric environmentalists are those of 'technocentric' environmentalists. These latter, whilst identifying similar problems to ecocentrics differ about the way in which progress can be achieved. They favour a rational approach to understanding the ecological basis of environmental problems and hold that it is a matter for efficient environmental management rather than a matter of questioning attitudes and values and the correctness of economic growth itself. Pepper (1984) like O'Riordan (1976), whilst recognising this two-fold classification of modern environmentalism to be simplistic when linked to political action, nevertheless goes on to suggest that technocentric attitudes became the dominant set of attitudes amongst official groups in society which exercise most power. Because technocentrics believe that progress is attainable by knowing and manipulating natural laws and working within the framework of economic laws, 'those who know most about these laws, the objective scientific 'experts', are those in whom trust should be placed when it comes to decision-making about the environment.' (Pepper, 1984 p.37). He further remarks that because of their relative ignorance, the public are disqualified from participation in this process at any level other than the most general.

This interpretation of environmentalism and the values and beliefs it is based upon has a number of consequences for the way in which official and voluntary groups responded to the growth in informal countryside recreation. Since mass participation in countryside recreation is by definition unorganised and its participants are not motivated by the same set of attitudes and values to the countryside as members of environmental groups, no organization represented its views. In theory the public sector purported to, as was evidenced by the national policies for 'Sport for All' and 'Countryside for All'. But even then, the Countryside Commission was restricted in its ability to promote a more egalitarian approach to countryside recreation because they were not able to take initiatives on their own and could only respond to requests for assistance initiated by local authorities.

Amongst local authorities a technocentric approach to countryside recreation prevailed especially amongst those with a strong rural constituency. Moreover, at the national and local level the public sector increasingly relied on the ability of planning and planners to provide a rational solution to the problem of leisure demand and environmental protection. In effect national and local public authorities concerned with countryside recreation came to be dominated by the same set of technocentric attitudes typical of the official groups Pepper identifies. Amongst providers, countryside recreation remained a problem to be managed rather than an opportunity for all people to benefit from. At the same time, most environmental groups who sought access to the countryside for recreation or to preserve the countryside, did so by pursuing proprietorial rights. As a result, the interests of informal, spontaneous outdoor recreation were placed outside the bargaining process unless public authorities chose to intervene deliberately on their behalf (see Chapter 5).

Countryside recreation and regional planning

As Mercer points out (Mercer, 1979), an agreed consensus existed amongst the planning profession during the 1960s about how leisure provision could best be made. Essentially, this amounted to a belief in the ability of mathematical and spatial models to provide optimum solutions to the matching of leisure demand with an adequate supply of facilities. Effective regional planning of resources and infra-structure would provide the required technological fix and sophisticated mathematical models, often those favoured by transport planners, would provide the means of achieving it. For the first time, leisure research became an essential part of the recreation planning process and over this period several major surveys of countryside recreation were conducted on a regional basis. They aimed to provide the detailed understanding of patterns of recreational activity in the belief that once the recreational system had been fully described and analysed, then the environmental threat posed by the fourth wave could be effectively managed.

Surveys such as Leisure in the North West (1967), the New Forest Study (1971) and the Study of Informal Recreation in South East England (SIRSEE) − (1976) which saw collaboration between the Greater London Council, the Countryside Commission, the Sports Council and the local authorities of the Home counties, are typical of the period (Countryside Commission, 1977a and b). Most studies incorporated surveys of participation, and included inventories of sites and facilities to establish recreational carrying capacities − often based on car-park size. Questionnaire surveys of visitors and residents were conducted in a belief that people, once consulted and their views accommodated within mathematical models like the gravity model, would behave rationally according to the physical laws upon which these models were based.

Many of these regional surveys of demand were prompted by the need to prepare Structure and Local Plans required by the Town and Country Planning Acts of 1968 and 1972. They were encouraged by the White Paper *Sport and Recreation* published in 1975 which firmly endorsed a social welfare approach to leisure (Department of the Environment, 1975b). As a result several county authorities and metropolitan authorities came to reappraise the recreational role of the countryside around towns and the contribution such areas could make to implementing socially motivated policies. By 1974 the Countryside Commission had raised the level of grants available for urban fringe Country Parks and several of the metropolitan authorities sought a more positive role for green belts in recreation provision rather than the containment role earlier policies had advocated. The formation of Regional Councils for Sport and Recreation in 1976 added weight to this approach.

These councils were responsible for developing regional recreation strategies to serve as a framework for the development of policies and proposals in the statutory Structure and Local Plans and to provide a forum for consultation between users and providers (Department of the Environment, 1976). Coalter et al. (1986) point out that these councils had no executive powers and in practice came to represent Sports Council priorities and monies rather than those of the Countryside Commission, but they did present an opportunity for fostering a more co-ordinated approach to provision at a time when outdoor recreation had become functionally, geographically and institutionally separate. The urban fringe, by virtue of its proximity to urban generated demand and its assumed accessibility to people from deprived urban areas, together with the opportunities it offered for bringing derelict land into beneficial use, became an integral part of the Councils' socially orientated recreation strategies.

A year after the foundation of these Regional Councils, an inter-departmental government committee set up to examine the future of the countryside – the Countryside Review Committee – also endorsed a community welfare approach to recreation and highlighted the socially beneficial role sites in urban fringe areas could play (1977). In practice however, it was often the Regional Councils supported by the metropolitan authorities who advanced prescriptive policies for green belts and urban fringes while shire counties, more concerned to protect their rate-payers interests and supported by the agricultural and environmental lobby, resisted them. Elson (1986) shows how authorities in the West Midlands, Manchester and Sheffield proposed priority areas for recreation in their Green Belt plans, such as green wedges, recreation areas and amenity zones only to find them whittled down by the policy consultation process and the Minister's later adjudication. In London and the South-East for example the Greater London Development Plan (1976) argued that:

'where studies of the Green Belt are not already in hand, they should be undertaken to see where it could be brought into recreational use, or access given to it.' (p.85)

The Home counties' response was to pursue policies which concentrated recreation facilities for use by Londoners into one or two honeypots such as the Lee Valley and Colne Valley Regional Parks and to upgrade existing open-spaces to Country Park status. The use of the honey-pot principle to deflect recreation pressure away from other countryside areas and from conflict with other land-uses, reflected technocentric attitudes and values as well as political and practical expediency. By 1979 the *Issues Report* prepared by the Greater London and South East Council for Sport and Recreation (GLSECSR, 1979) saw a renewed emphasis again on the scientifically neutral and value-free concept of capacity as the basis upon which any additional provision should be based. This despite the fact that as early as 1971 Law and Perry's study of demand and supply (1971) had demonstrated the spatial disparity in provision which existed on a sectoral basis around London and the inaccessibility of much of the Green Belt to people living in the 'most deprived' areas of central London. A state of affairs that was reinforced by Fitton's detailed analysis of demand and supply (Fitton, 1976) and Ferguson and Munton's (1978, 1979) independent study (Figure 3.5). Moreover, the tendency for surveys to focus on peak demand measured at popular sites which had latterly also become 'more vulnerable' to damage because of their newly designated nature conservation interest, for example Kynance Cove in Cornwall, parts of the Pennine Way in the Peak District and Box Hill in Surrey, served to suggest that this was typical of all the countryside and all environments.

The preoccupation of regional planning with strategic issues rather than with detailed studies of both latent and effective recreational demand and their reluctance to examine the variable capacities of a range of sites to accommodate use, emphasized the view that recreation was a problem to be managed. Together with the dominance of technocentric attitudes, amongst planners this view prevailed even when central government in its White Paper *'Sport and Recreation'* (Department of the Environment, 1975b) encouraged authorities to think otherwise.

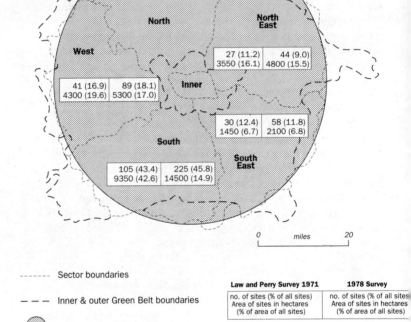

Figure 3.5: Countryside sites in the London Green Belt 1971 and 1978
Source: Ferguson and Munton, 1978

Limited resources and resourcefulness

By the mid-1970s financial considerations assumed a new importance which consolidated a 'managerialist' approach to public spending. A reduction in funding and staff, together with a growing realization that a positive approach to recreation provision and landscape enhancement were beyond the scale and scope of strategic planning, saw the Countryside Commission promote a new approach based on 'Countryside Management' (Countryside Commission, 1974, Bromley, 1990). They invested considerable energy and effort in promoting management experiments as a practical means of resolving some of the problems which mass participation in countryside recreation provoked.

First used in the uplands of Snowdonia in 1969 where conflicts over public access by visitors had arisen with other land owners in the National Park and used successively at the coast in 1976 and urban fringe in 1981, this approach can be interpreted as a technocentric approach to the resolution of environmental problems that operates 'outside' the planning system (see Chapter 7). It did not seek to question why the conflicts had arisen in the first place. In practice too, the approach based on a partnership with local authorities and the voluntary sector provided a pragmatic solution to the Commission's own deteriorating financial circumstances. By developing a partnership approach which included the voluntary sector as well, countryside management also came to mesh well with the new thinking which accompanied the election of a Conservative government in 1979.

At a time when the principles of a free-market economy lead to the encouragement of private ownership, cost-effectiveness, and voluntarism, this partnership approach continued to gain ground throughout the 1980s. However, it also marked a shift in thinking away from a preoccupation with site-based approaches to a consideration of how the Commission's dual responsibilities for conservation and recreation could be achieved in the wider countryside. A reorientation in emphasis which the findings of successive recreation surveys conducted in the 1980s were to justify.

Emerging issues and Recreation 2000

In retrospect, the challenge presented by the leisure revolution of the period 1960–80 seems to have been interpreted rather differently by the two national agencies responsible for planning and providing sport and recreation. The Countryside Commission interpreted demand as a problem to be managed and over the two decades up to 1978, Fitton (1978) recalls that 'although facilitating as well as controlling policies have been evident in the development of countryside recreation strategy ... it can be justifiably argued that the latter have predominated.' By contrast the Sports Council interpreted rising demand as a positive indication that society as a whole could benefit from increased participation in sport. The 'Sport for All' policy launched in 1972 and its various successors, (See McIntosh and Charlton, 1985), was a policy of motivation designed to promote sport as a desirable social concept but it also tapped a change in attitude to sport in the community as a whole. First encountered in America where it became fashionable to be fit – sport acquired a new attraction among prosperous sections of society and when linked to the Olympic movement, the need to promote excellence in sport also acquired a new sense of national urgency. The tenacity with which the Sports Council pursued these social policies through into the 1980s is in marked contrast to the rather more pragmatic policies adopted by the Countryside Commission in which social policies have played a minor part (Coalter et al., 1986).

One explanation for these differing responses can be found in terms of the numbers of people who took part and the geographical base of their respective constituencies. Over 84% of the population visited the countryside in a year whereas fewer than 10% participated in active sport. Given this level of countryside visiting, a strong promotional stance by the Commission might well have been deemed to be irresponsible especially under the straitened financial circumstances of the late 1970s and early 1980s (Mays, 1982). On the other hand, a more promotional approach by the Sports Council was deemed to be more acceptable amongst urban authorities, but even then it achieved greater acceptance when used to promote excellence in sport rather than in widening the base of community participation.

A further explanation for these differing approaches, however, lies in the historical specificity of events and in the technocentric attitudes which came to dominate those public authorities best positioned to promote a more socially-orientated approach to countryside recreation provision. Throughout this period the Countryside Commission never seriously questioned the rationale for its involvement in recreation provision until 1985, when it embarked on its first major policy review. In announcing this review – *Recreation 2000*, the Commission acknowledged that the mounting concern expressed by environmental groups about the damaging activities of productive rural land-uses once thought to be benign – agriculture and forestry – had deflected much of the Commissions' energies into activities which concerned the conservation of landscapes rather than promoting enjoyment of the countryside. It also admitted that the 'way we help people enjoy the countryside has stayed largely unchanged since we were established in 1968' and suggested that in the mean time 'there had been a major shift in public interest in, and expectations of, the countryside.' (*Recreation 2000*, Countryside Commission, 1987b).

Clearly, by the mid-1980s the social, economic and political context within which countryside recreation was taking place had changed sufficiently to warrant a major review of the Countryside Commission's national policies. It is of some significance therefore, that when the Commission offered its preliminary proposals for public consultation these were entitled *'Enjoying the Countryside'* (Countryside Commission, 1987c). This new found emphasis on enjoyment rather than containment suggested a new sensitivity and awareness of what countryside recreation means and appeared to mark a new phase in the history of countryside recreation in which the interests and concerns of the wider public were to be addressed directly. Several issues arise from this policy review and are discussed here under two broad categories, issues relating to demand and those concerned with access and accessibility.

Demand at the national level

Even before 1985 there were signs that the demand for countryside recreation was no longer growing at the rate it had during the first half of the 1970s, but, it was not until 1982 that firm evidence of a slowing down in growth was reported. (Countryside Commission, 1982). At that time, a review of participation in informal recreation based on the findings of the first two national surveys of countryside recreation revealed a 22% decline in the numbers of people who had visited the countryside between 1977 and 1980 and a fall in the number of trips made, from 101 million in 1977 to 81 million in 1980. Other evidence of declining demand was also reported from an analysis of leisure day-trips recorded by the English Tourist Board (ETB) for the years 1981 and 1982. In this period the volume of day trips fell by 6% but a 14% decline was recorded for drives and tours in the countryside in general and a 13% drop in outdoor trips of a non-commercial nature (ETB, 1983). Trends in outdoor sports in the same period showed a similar decline (MacIntosh and Charlton, 1985). An overall rise in participation rates up to 1977 was followed by a decline amongst most participating groups and a particularly steep decline was recorded amongst unemployed people. Participation amongst students and members of the armed forces – groups for which special facilities were available, ran counter to this trend (Figure 3.6).

Such surveys suggested that the phenomenal growth in outdoor recreation which had been experienced in the post-war period had indeed been fuelled by rising prosperity amongst society as a whole and that when the national economy entered a depression, as it did during the late 1970s, so participation in outdoor recreation also declined. Why this should be the case however remained unclear because both car-ownership and holiday entitlement continued to increase over this same period (HMSO, 1986). Moreover, subsequent national surveys of countryside recreation conducted in 1984, 1985 and 1986 suggested that even when several economic indicators improved in the

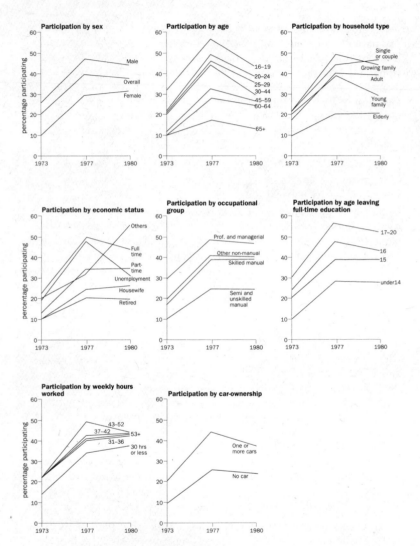

Figure 3.6: Participation in outdoor sport
Source: Sports Council, 1985

mid-1980s, this improvement was not reflected in the percentage of people who participated in visits to the countryside unless – as was the case in 1984 – this was accompanied by a fine summer. By 1986, the percentage of people who had visited the countryside in the previous month had not returned to the levels recorded for 1977.

Such uncertainty about the relationship between the performance of the national economy and countryside recreation suggested that for the first time since the war, public agencies and private landlords apparently no longer needed to view countryside recreation as a 'fourth wave' spreading out across the countryside and recreation policies which had been based on the assumption that mass participation in recreation was a threat, could be revised. What kind of policies should replace them was far from clear because other aspects of demand had changed too.

Shifts in recreational tastes

Although demand at a national level appeared to have stabilized, rather more problematic was the extent to which recreation tastes were changing in concert with both a restructuring of employment opportunities and work practices and with changing residential patterns. By the mid-1980s the countryside had become a favoured location for industries in the service sector – one of the most rapidly growing sectors of the economy, and a favoured residential location especially for the more prosperous population of the South East region. These economic and social changes suggested that some areas of the countryside would be subjected to new recreational demands, partly because the population of several rural communities was increasing and partly because the recreational tastes of new residents themselves were changing. Taken together these changes suggested that demands for improved access to the countryside would increase and the nature of demand might also change if changing recreational tastes contested the dominant countryside aesthetic. For example, studies suggested that membership of some outdoor sports organizations such as rambling, canoeing and mountaineering was continuing to grow (Figure 3.7) and other novel, non-rural recreational pursuits such as hang-gliding, parascending, hot air ballooning, and war-games were making new demands for access to land, water and the air (Centre for Leisure Research, 1986). So, although overall participation in countryside recreation might have stabilized, shifts in recreational tastes were likely to mean that new demands for access would be made of the countryside (Sidaway, 1985).

Where and why people visit

Uncertainties about the nature of recreational demand were further compounded when other aspects of recreational behaviour were examined. Successive national surveys of countryside recreation had shown that the destinations of the overwhelming majority of countryside trips lay in the un-managed or wider countryside with its fields,

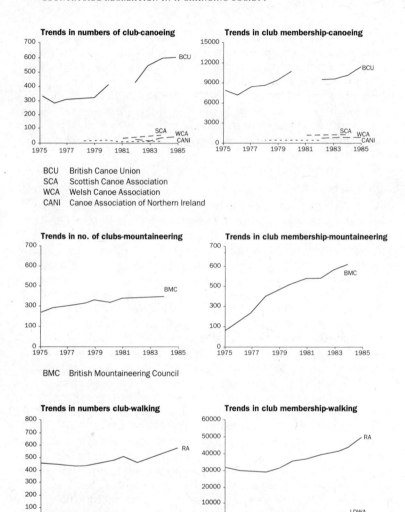

BCU   British Canoe Union
SCA   Scottish Canoe Association
WCA   Welsh Canoe Association
CANI   Canoe Association of Northern Ireland

BMC   British Mountaineering Council

RA   Ramblers' Association
LDWA   Long Distance Walkers Association

Figure 3.7: Trends in selected outdoor activities 1975–1985
Source: Sports Council, 1986

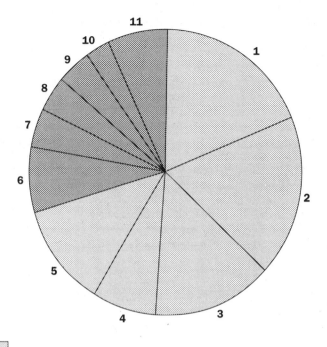

Unmanaged countryside	1 Drives, outings, picnics	19%
	2 Long walks	18%
	3 Visiting friends, relatives	14%
	4 Sea coast	8%
	5 Informal sport	12%
Managed countryside	6 Organised sport	7%
	7 Pick your own	4%
	8 Historic buildings	4%
	9 Country parks	4%
	10 Watched sport	3%
	11 Others	7%

Figure 3.8: Countryside trips, destinations and activities
Source: Countryside Commission, National Survey of Countryside Recreation 1984

farms and villages. Only a minority of trips were made to sites specifically managed for countryside recreation such as Country Parks, Picnic Sites, Public Open Spaces and National Trust properties (Figure 3.8). Such evidence suggested that earlier policies which had been designed to deflect recreational pressure away from National Parks by providing alternative attractions such as Country Parks, did not reflect how the countryside was being used. It also called into question the cost-effectiveness of the Commission's policy of resource allocation which gave priority to grant aid for Country Parks rather than to other kinds of services available to visitors.

Other questions were also prompted by this evidence. What kind of enjoyment do people get from visiting the wider countryside and why do managed sites apparently fail to provide the enjoyment people want? Are managed sites used less because people do not know where they are or because they are less attractive than the wider countryside? Providing answers to these kinds of questions involves a close examination of people's motivations, attitudes and values. When coupled with the uncertainty about what form future recreational demand will take, they also suggest that there is a real discrepancy between what countryside recreation means to the general public and what it means to those individuals and groups in society who are in a position to influence where, when and how the countryside is enjoyed – landowners, public authorities and national agencies. If public intervention in countryside recreation is to better reflect what people want, then studies of peoples attitudes, expectations and values are required and particularly if socially motivated policies are to be justified.

Who participates?

When analyzed by social class, income level and economic activity, participants in countryside recreation are drawn from all sections of society and in absolute terms the volume of trips made by clerical and skilled manual workers is higher than other groups because they are more numerous in the population as a whole (Fitton, 1979). Even so, a consistent feature of national and regional recreational surveys is the fact that people who are better-off in terms of income level, education level, and car-ownership, visit the countryside more frequently than people who are less well-off (Countryside Commission, 1980b, and 1985). Overall some 17% of the population make 68% of the trips and most of these people are drawn from the higher socio-economic groups (Figure 3.9).

Viewed in this way, countryside recreation does indeed appear to be the indulgence of the middle classes. For example, in 1984 people who lived in households with access to a car were almost three times as likely to visit the countryside as people who did not have access to a car. Similarly, members of professional and managerial households, and by definition high income households, were almost three times as likely to the visit the countryside as people on low incomes and people in households where the head of the household was unemployed. Because social grouping is itself correlated with income level, car-ownership, holiday entitlement and the number of years spent in education, it is not possible to disentangle their separate effects on participation. Hence, it is difficult to know whether people who are well-off go to the countryside more often because they like to spend

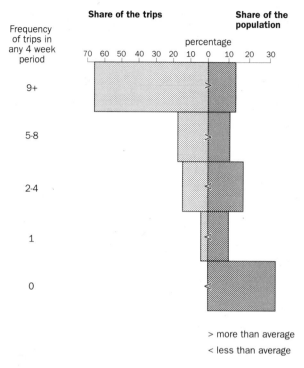

Figure 3.9: Trip-making as a percentage of the total population
Source: Countryside Commission, National Survey of Countryside Recreation 1984

their leisure time in this way, because their personal circumstances – including where they live and how well-informed they are about their local area – mean that it is easier for them to get into the countryside, or because the kind of recreational provision favoured by providers meshes well with their own recreational tastes. Conversely, people who are less well-off, such as manual and semi-skilled workers may only visit the countryside infrequently because they prefer to do other things in their leisure time, because they are poor and their personal circumstances – including ignorance and lack of available recreational opportunities, make it more difficult for them to get into the countryside or because what is provided is not what they want.

Disentangling these complex relationships in which relative levels of prosperity, leisure preferences and accessibility of the countryside all impinge on visiting behaviour have preoccupied leisure researchers for decades but, the requirement to understand these relationships is

63

particularly important if socially-motivated policies for countryside recreation are to be justified and implemented.

Rationales for socially motivated policies

At the time of the Countryside Commission's review of recreation policies, several pointers suggested that a growing proportion of the population were experiencing, or were likely to experience, lives which were leisure-poor. First, an ageing process in the population as a whole meant that elderly people would represent a larger proportion of the population than in previous decades. Second, a trend towards early retirement meant that an increasing number of people were seeking to enjoy the rewards of a life spent in work before advancing infirmity prevented their partners and themselves from doing so. Third, structural changes in the economy had also seen the number of unemployed people rise to well above two million during the 1980s. Precipitated by a decline in heavy industry and exacerbated by a poor performance in the manufacturing sector, the 1980s saw many skilled and unskilled employees out of work. Fourth, an increase in the number of single parent households, highlighted another group in society who are known to encounter real difficulties in securing any leisure time, including visits to the countryside. Fifth, although little research had been conducted into the leisure behaviour and preferences of different ethnic groups, there was sufficient circumstantial evidence from household and visitor surveys to suggest that existing policies were not addressing their needs. The review of recreation policies provided an opportunity to pursue socially-motivated policies directed towards these constituencies, not least because the phenomenal growth in demand had levelled off and countryside recreation could be regarded as an opportunity to enhance people's lives and not as a threat to the interests of countryside landowners.

Access and accessibility

Central to a reappraisal of what countryside recreation means in modern society and the role the public sector might play in providing what people want, is the question of accessibility. Earlier chapters have shown that proprietorial rights convey upon rural landowners the power to determine when, where and what recreational activities occur in the countryside. They have also shown that successive attempts by recreational organizations to persuade the government of the day to improve public rights of access to the countryside, have failed to alter the supremacy of proprietorial rights (Cherry, 1985). In choosing not to pursue a new Access Charter at the time of their review of policies, the Commission implicitly accepted the continued domination of proprietorial rights for determining how accessible the countryside is to the public. Instead, the Commission chose to focus their attention on bringing into beneficial use the existing Rights of Way network and to continue to negotiate for freer public access to countryside areas through Access and Management Agreements. This conciliatory approach brings only marginal improvements in public access and accepts the correctness of market-based principles for determining how any improvements in access might be gained. In this latter respect, such approaches seemed to mesh well with the dominant political and economic policies of the government of the day and with the changing economic fortunes of rural landowners who were beginning to reasses their capital assets in the face of declining farm incomes. Whether or not such approaches also reflect the views of recreational groups and the general public is less certain and requires closer examination.

History reveals that for some groups gaining access to the countryside is a matter of principle – a right of citizenship to be secured only by changing the legal rights of landowners. On the other hand, many recreationists are prepared to negotiate access to the countryside through the market place although the terms they are prepared to accept and the degree of tenure they secure, varies considerably. Determining how accessible the countryside is regarded to be, therefore depends not only upon people's willingness to accept that recreation is only to be experienced through membership of an organization, but also upon a willingness to accept the free-market as the primary mechanism for achieving access. Some people, for example, may regard the question of access to be a matter for selective public intervention rather than universal legislation so that the interests of particular activities are protected or access is secured to particular environments close to where demand lies. Justification for public intervention in countryside recreation whether it be instrumental (land reform), facilitatory (access agreements, countryside management) or residuary in nature (directed to particular activities or areas not served by the market) is therefore likely to depend critically upon public attitudes to countryside access and a willingness to use market mechanisms to secure it. Chapter 4 examines the complex relationship between public attitudes to the countryside and recreational behaviour. It also examines how attitudes to public access vary amongst users of the countryside and groups who control access to it.

65

Conclusion

The period 1960–1987 proved to be a complex one in the history of countryside recreation. Rising popular demand saw countryside recreation established as a separate arena of activity for central and local government. However the institutionalization of outdoor recreation through the Countryside Commission and Sports Council, saw countryside recreation increasingly defined as the quiet enjoyment of open countryside and not enjoyment of the diverse range of social and environmental experiences demand suggested. Even when the spectre of enforced unemployment, early retirement and an ageing population pointed to the growing number of people who would experience poor quality lives, public sector policies for countryside recreation seemed remarkably elitist and selective. Amongst shire counties, private landed interests and a vociferous environmental lobby ensured that public sector policies remained concerned with containing where demand fell rather than with improving the quality of people's lives.

The Countryside Commission did not remain impervious to the changing social and cultural context of countryside recreation and its policy review conducted in the late 1980s was a genuine attempt to address these emerging issues. Indeed the range of policies finally adopted by the Commission in 1987 attempt to address the multiple recreational needs of a more diverse constituency than earlier policies, but the mechanisms chosen to pursue these policies remain just as constrained by the laws and customs attached to proprietorial rights as earlier ones. In consequence, the policies do little to contest the dominant ideology of the countryside aesthetic or to promote a new culture of provision better able to meet people's expectations of what countryside recreation means. Justification for this conclusion is provided in later chapters which explore how effective a variety of facilitatory and residuary approaches have been at improving access and accessibility and at contesting the appropriateness of particular recreational activities for inclusion in the countryside.

4

Attitudes to the countryside and to public access

....

Introduction

Earlier chapters have shown how countryside recreation has come to play an important role in people's leisure activities and how people's expectations and experiences of the countryside are intimately bound up with the way society is organized. If we accept this interpretation, it is relevant to ask how people's enjoyment of the countryside today reflects conditions in modern society. Moreover, at a time when the agricultural imperative for retaining farming as the dominant land-use in the countryside has come under increasing attack from a variety of organisations and interests, it is pertinent to ask what the countryside means to people who seek to enjoy the countryside for outdoor recreation. It is helpful to know for example, what significance is attached to those outstanding environments successive legislation has sought to protect for purposes of outdoor recreation and to those ordinary, farmed and settled landscapes which receive little statutory protection. For, although there can be little doubt that the countryside is highly valued by all kinds of people, it is less clear how environmental attitudes and recreational preferences are related to the recreational use of the countryside as a whole. Several national surveys for example suggest that countryside recreation has selective appeal to different groups in society (Curry and Comely, 1986). Whether these differential participation levels are class-based or reflect other aspects of society and locality is difficult to determine. Moreover, it is difficult to know whether the the kinds of provision society has made for countryside recreation, provide equal benefits to all those who seek to enjoy the countryside.

Answers to these kinds of questions require an examination of people's attitudes to the countryside, their motivations for visiting the countryside and reasons for engaging in some outdoor activities and not others. By structuring enquiry in this way, it is possible for example, to discover whether the countryside is enjoyed as a holistic experience that is commonly-shared or is a set of separate and distinctive experiences that can only be gained by undertaking particular activities in particular settings or at particular destinations. Further, since several surveys show that some social groups participate in countryside recreation more frequently than others, studies of recreational attitudes and preferences can explore whether particular kinds of recreational facilities and environmental settings have selective appeal to different social groups.

Much of the evidence about the selective appeal of recreational and environmental preferences derived from questionnaire surveys is tantalizing in its ambiguity and their findings are difficult to relate to either the pattern and type of provision available or to how accessible facilities are to different social groups. Hence, they need to be treated with caution (Veal, 1980). Equally, analysis conducted at an aggregate level and based on social group or occupational status cannot adequately explain *why* people participate or *why* some facilities and locations are preferred to others.

In order to address these questions much of the discussion which follows draws upon the findings of qualitative studies which have been designed to explore people's attitudes and motivations. These studies show that differing ideologies of the countryside influence how the countryside is both defined and enjoyed. In particular, they show that the very many organizations which have an interest in the recreational use of the countryside do not share the same view about what constitutes the 'appropriate recreational use of the countryside'. Furthermore, when these various attitudes to appropriate use are linked to alternative views about the role of proprietorial rights as the legal mechanism for providing access, organized groups adopt different strategies for gaining access to the countryside. As a result, although most discussions about the future of the countryside take for granted the fact that the countryside is an unexceptional term and means the same thing to all parties, in-depth studies reveal that it is not possible to talk about one countryside, one way of enjoying the countryside or one access lobby. In contemporary society, as in earlier periods, the countryside and its enjoyment is culturally and socially defined both by those who seek access to the countryside and by those who own and manage it.

Recreational preferences – the evidence from national surveys

Household surveys reveal intriguing patterns of visitor behaviour when analyzed by social group. For example, Curry and Comley's (1986) detailed analysis of National Survey of Countryside Recreation and the General Household Surveys for three separate years (1973, 77, 83) shows that there is a clear gradation of participation in country-side recreation by occupational group for any one year (Table 4.1). Apart from watching outdoor sports and fishing, there appears to be a greater level of countryside activity as occupational status increases. They provide a detailed analysis of the relative preferences for differ-ent types of recreational activity by social groups based on the 1984 National Survey of Countryside Recreation (NSCR). Table 4.2 illus-trates preferences for different countryside recreation activities by social group and the ranking it suggests is corroborated by a chi-square analysis using social groups A/B, C1/C2 and D/E/Eu grouped together to see if there was any positive relationship between activities and groups. This analysis suggests that proportionately more visits are made to historic buildings and to Nature Reserves by social groups A/B than would be expected if there were no relationship between social group and activity and a lower use by groups D/E/Eu. This rela-tionship is reversed when participation in fishing is analysed. Social groups C1/C2 reveal a higher than expected number of visits to zoos and safari parks – a preference that Fitton (1978) had remarked upon from his manipulation of the NSCR surveys of 1973 and 1977. Fitton also suggests that attractions which promote social interaction such as country pubs and safari parks prove to be more attractive to lower status occupational groups, although this is an assumption rather than a view based on the attitudes of respondents.

In contrast to household surveys which record what people say they do, surveys of visitors reveal expressed demand. Visitor surveys con-ducted at different recreation sites in the countryside (Elson, 1979, Harrison, 1983) show that people from all social groups visit the full range of facilities and that no consistent relationship exists between the type of site and social group. In other words, provision located in particular sites whether this is of an informal or more organised nature, has wide appeal right across the social spectrum.

The evidence from visitor surveys undertaken at more commercial attractions is equally equivocal. For example, a survey of 1540 adults over 15 years old undertaken at several commercial leisure attraction in the summer of 1985 (Applied Leisure Marketing Ltd.,1985) exam-ined the social profile of visitors to 'cultural' attractions such as muse-ums and historic buildings, to 'nature' attractions such as zoos,

69

Table 4.1: The General Household Survey: Participation in countryside recreation activities by socio-economic group – 1973, 1977, 1984

All figures for adults of 16 and over in Great Britain.
Percentage in each activity in previous 4 weeks (except 1973 – figures for whole year)

Recreation activity	Total	Prof-essional	Employers and managers	Inter-mediatel non-man	Junior non-manual	Skilled manual	Semi-skilled manual	Unskilled	Never worked	Full-time student
1973										
Active outdoor sports	17	35	25	24	17	19	11	8	6	39
Watching outdoor sports	10	11	12	11	9	14	8	7	1	16
Open-air outings*	21	31	26	30	25	20	16	13	12	21
Visits to historic buildings/ museums/zoos	9	19	13	17	11	6	5	3	3	5
Golf	2	8	7	3	2	2	1	0	n/A	3
Fishing	2	2	3	2	1	4	1	2	N/A	2
Walking (2+ miles)	17	29	23	27	20	15	12	10	N/A	22
1977										
Open-air outings*	22	19	20	19	14	14	11	14	N/A	16
Visits to historic buildings/ museums/zoos	23	18	23	15	11	8	6	20	N/A	13
1984										
Walking (2+ miles)	19	30	24	27	22	16	15	13	N/A	19
Golf	2	8	6	3	1	2	1	0	N/A	3
Fishing	2	1	3	1	1	4	2	1	N/A	4
Cycling	2	5	1	2	2	1	1	2	N/A	6

* This category may include outings to urban parks and the coast as well as the countryside
Sources (OPCS, 1976, 1979, 1982, 1985; CSO, 1982)

wildlife parks and gardens, to 'theme parks' with 'white-knuckle' attractions, and to 'general recreation facilities' such as leisure parks, steam railways,and model villages. Cultural attractions proved to be most attractive to A/B/C1 social groups, while the theme parks appealed most strongly to social group C2 and showed less appeal to higher social groups A/B. When 'nature attractions' are classified to include gardens as well as safari parks and zoos, the selective appeal

Table 4.2: The 1984 NSCR: Social group preferences for different countryside recreation activities
Source: Curry and Comley, 1986

Percentage of people in each group participating: Rank order

	Most 1	2	3	4	5	6	Fewest 7
Visited the sea coast or cliff tops	A	B	C1	C2	D	E	EU
Visited historic buildings, stately homes or museums, gardens or parks	B	A	C1	C2	D	E	EU
Visited country parks	B	C1	A	C2	D	E	EU
Visited zoos, safari or wildlife parks	**C1**	**B**	C2	A	D	EU	E
Visited nature reserves	B	A	C1	C2	D	E	EU
Been on drives, outings, picnics	B	A	C1	C2	D	E	EU
Been on long walks, rambles or hikes	A	B	C1	C2	D	EU	E
Outdoor sporting activities*	A	B	C1	C2	D	E	EU
Visited friends or relatives in the countryside	A	B	C1	C2	D	E	EU
Conservation or recreation work	A	B	C1	C2	D	**E**	**EU**
Picking your own fruit, etc.	B	A	C1	C2	D	E	EU

* includes fishing, hunting, horseriding, shooting. Bold type indicates equal percentages

identified in Curry and Comley's analysis is not sustained. Other general recreation facilities prove to be slightly more attractive to social groups D/E but, for A/B and C2 groups, the social profile of visitors at these sites matched the national profile.

As is the case with the findings from visitor surveys conducted at countryside sites which provide few facilities, the study of commercial leisure attractions suggests that people from all social groups are attracted to them. Equally, these studies confirm there is a willingness to pay for some recreational facilities across all social groups. In practice therefore, the findings of surveys of participation are equivocal about any consistent relationship which might suggest that certain recreational environments and facilities appeal to particular social groups. Most surveys emphasize that people in all social groups enjoy a variety of natural and commercial attractions when they visit the countryside.

In a similar vein, studies which have examined the relationship between the kinds of recreational activities people engage in (active and non-active) and particular benefits associated with the countryside, fail to discriminate between different activity groups (Centre for leisure Research, 1986). The benefits of countryside recreation were perceived to be similar amongst all groups whether respondents were committed walkers, people who engaged in active sport or those who enjoyed informal activities. Hence, although there is some limited evidence from household surveys which suggests that there is a relationship between social group and participation in the countryside recreation, the perceived benefits of the countryside are equally valued by different visitor and activity groups. Moreover, such surveys and their analysis provide little insight into *why* particular attractions or activities may have selective appeal. For these reasons, it is instructive to examine the findings of qualitative studies which have explored leisure preferences and environmental values.

The popular appeal of the countryside – qualitative studies

Over the last few years a number of qualitative studies have been completed in leisure research (see Fitton, 1979, Mostyn, 1979, Operation Gateway, 1984, and the Qualitative Consultancy, 1986) and by the Sheffield group working with women (Green et al. 1987), Harrison et al. (1987) working with several inner city residents and by the Centre for Leisure Research during their major study of *Access to the Countryside for Recreation and Sport* (1986). Each of these studies had a different overall objective and they also differed in terms of the qualitative methods used to implement them. Of central concern to them all however, is an attempt to reveal people's attitudes and values as they relate to several facets of leisure activities and to explore how these values differ amongst recreationists, providers and those 'gatekeepers' who plan and control recreational opportunities in the countryside. Within the broad scope of countryside recreation two related themes are addressed here namely:

▓ the environmental attitudes and values of particular user groups, especially those attitudes held by people who have no recent tradition of visiting the countryside (Harrison et al. 1986 and the Qualitative Consultancy, 1986)

▓ the attitudes and values of organized groups with an interest in outdoor recreation and those of the 'gatekeepers' of countryside resources (Centre for Leisure Research, 1986).

The former demonstrate that even commonly-used terms like countryside and countryside recreation have different meanings to different people and the latter that there is not one access lobby but several.

Both illustrate how differing ideologies of the countryside influence why some kinds of recreational activities and not others are regarded as appropriate in the countryside.

Attitudes of infrequent visitors to the countryside

Two recent studies have explicitly set out to understand people's motivations for visiting the countryside and their attitudes to it. The first conducted by the Qualitative Consultancy (1986) for the Countryside Commission used 12 once-only discussion groups with people drawn from rural, suburban and urban areas in England and Wales (Philips and Ashcroft, 1987). The other study conducted by the author and others (Harrison et al. 1986a and b) used four, in-depth discussion groups held with people drawn from different neighbourhoods in Greenwich – a middle London Borough. In both studies, the members of the groups were drawn from a wide cross-section of the local community and not from particular interest or activity groups. The studies also focused on the views and attitudes of informal recreationists who visit the countryside rarely or infrequently (Figure 4.1).

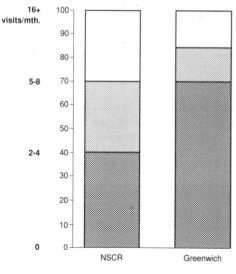

Figure 4.1: Frequency of visits to the country-side: National Survey and Greenwich sample compared
Source: Harrison et al., 1986b

In the Greenwich study two groups were recruited from white, working-class communities based on Thamesmead and Plumstead; a third was composed solely of Asian women and a fourth group was recruited from a middle-class suburb in Eltham. Members of this latter group visited the countryside more frequently than members of the other three groups. The groups met for an hour and a half each over a period of six weeks and during that time people came to discuss their experiences of the countryside and other open areas such as urban parks and open spaces, and to explore their more deeply-held environmental attitudes and values. A full discussion of the use of in-depth groups for researching environmental values is provided in Burgess et al. 1988 a and b.

The common finding from these studies is that the 'countryside' provides enormous pleasure to most people even though people may not visit it very frequently. The Greenwich study also revealed that the term countryside itself means different things to different people and that people's enjoyment of the countryside also varies. Pleasurable experiences enjoyed in the countryside are sought in a variety of different countryside environments and social contexts. As revealed through these discussions, countryside recreation is neither confined to particular environments set aside for recreation nor is enjoying the countryside restricted to the solitary and self conscious contemplation of peace and quiet which is often used as a metaphor for countryside recreation in public debates. In addition, both studies provide insights into why the countryside holds little appeal to a minority of people.

The pleasures of being in the countryside

The two studies reinforce the commonly-held view that much of the pleasure of visits to the countryside stems from encounters with the living world of the countryside. With its wonderful array of sounds, smells, sights and feelings, the countryside provides a range of active and sensual pleasures that are not the merely passive events so many questionnaire surveys suggest. Being out in the countryside and away from the burden of urban life brings pleasure in itself, but importantly too, active encounters with the natural world bring particular pleasure. Many people described their experiences of the countryside in terms of those occasions when their senses were heightened. For example in the Greenwich study Patricia explains:

'...this feeling of the downy grass that's springing on the top of the chalky cliffs. It's a bit eerie actually because it does move as you move.'

and Frank's description of an organised, nightime walk in the Surrey countryside:

'...you have a torch and it's a bit eerie... There's no light there...pick out owl's eyes and funny things... I just turned out my torch, and I was creeping up behind people... There doesn't seem to be anything there, but there is!' (T2.1911-68).[1]

This active involvement with the natural world of the countryside is a far cry from the stereotypical views of the countryside as attractive landscapes to be enjoyed essentially for their aesthetic appeal. It is also far removed from the concept of nature as a laboratory to be studied, recorded and dissected by those who know best. Informal countryside recreation involves the pleasures of encounters with the living world of the countryside that are not passive, self-conscious or studious. Rather they are active, spontaneous, and naive encounters. For example Viv describes the first time she had visited the countryside in the winter:

'It was in Kingston, Canterbury. Very barren in a way. Like the soil was very limey and I've never actually seen churned up limey soil before... there wasn't much growing... As we got out of that, it became very peaty and boggy and then much greener, which was really nice. But it was the first time I'd been out actually into the country and had experienced such a deadness about everything, 'cos there were no leaves on anything. In fact all the trees were pretty dead. But it was still nice. It beats walking along the railway line here, I can assure you.' (P2. 432–455).

This description stands in stark contrast to the idealized and intellectualized view of the countryside used in so many public debates which depicts countryside as outstanding landscapes rather than ordinary countryside (Penning-Rowsell and Lowenthal, 1986). Viv's account also highlights the importance of the agricultural countryside. Indeed, for many people in the Greenwich groups, the working countryside with its farms and villages, fields and pubs had wide appeal. The romantic appeal of the working countryside is well expressed when Diane reveals:

'I quite like to see working land. Like when there's tractors ploughing it over and then you see the flock of gulls behind it and then you can see the tractor disappear right into the distance and then come all the way back again. And later, when all the barley's growing or whatever they decide to plant. Then the harvesters when they harvest it. I like to see things like that.' (Diane, P4. 1153–8).

---

1. T2 refers to the second meeting of the Thamesmead group, lines 1911–68. The transcripts of the group discussions have been deposited in the ESRC Data Archive, Essex

Through the extended life of the Greenwich discussion groups strong contrasts emerged between those people who wanted the peace and quiet of the unmanaged countryside and those people who enjoyed the farmed and settled countryside with its variety of attractions. For a number of middle-class people the wild landscapes of the upland areas or the undeveloped coast had most appeal but for others the agricultural countryside has special appeal too. The contrasts between an agricultural countryside and the attractions of moorland are clearly revealed by Elaine:

'The thing about moorland areas is the feeling that... you can walk anywhere. You have access to... everywhere you can see. If you can reach there on foot, you can get there. You can scramble up that cliff. You can paddle in that stream. You can walk across that bog. Whereas if you see a field, even if you have to cross the sheep field in order to get to the moorland on the other side, you are conscious that it's somebody else's land. That you must be very careful to close the gate behind you... I mean of course if it's land that's growing crops you wouldn't dream of setting foot in it because that is somebody else's land. You would enjoy it only as a visual thing... like a nice church in the distance and a little hamlet and whatever... But while you can enjoy the views, like looking at a painting by somebody else, it's not yours to trespass on. Whereas the moorland or the sort of National Park areas you feel free that you have access to that. And um, that you can actually just go – you can go right into it! It's like going into the picture... you can walk into the moorland. You can actually go in and you can possess it. You go to the hilltop and all that you can see is mine, as it were.' (E3.1462–86)

For many middle-class people in the groups, genuine countryside experiences could only be gained in moorland and wilderness-like areas where they had freedom to roam and where they could 'possess' the landscape through their experiences within it. In this sense many of those same pleasures enjoyed by the nineteenth century romantics like Wordsworth and Coleridge are also enjoyed by some people in modern society.

This contrast between the appeal of the farmed countryside and that of the more natural landscapes of the uplands was also revealed by the discussions held with Asian women. These women's experiences of the British countryside varied. One or two had travelled widely in Britain, while others had only been on occasional trips. For them all however, the descriptions of the British countryside focused on a working countryside in which animals, friendly people, farms – including pick your own farms, fresh air and little pollution figured prominently. The concept of the countryside as 'wilderness' has no significance for them, in part because their own childhoods had been spent in the agricultural countryside of a distant land but in part too because we know from other studies such as that of Nash (1967) and Thomas (1984), that the concept of 'wilderness' is itself culturally and socially constructed.

Strong differences also emerged in terms of the company people found acceptable. Many middle-class people only wanted to share their countryside experiences with close companions but, others sought the company of friends and family and much of their own enjoyment of the countryside also stemmed from seeing other people having fun. By contrast, the absence of unsympathetic 'others': strangers, crowds and other intrusive reminders of city life, is crucial to some people's enjoyment. The dilemma this poses, is forcefully recognized by Mary when she recalls her experience in Scotland:

'I was at the Queen's View, the other side of Pitlochry, and I think it was the most beautiful serene scenery I have ever witnessed and I could have stood and just stood. And I hated the people that were standing looking at the same time as me, because I didn't think they fitted in. But there again, had I not gone by road, I wouldn't have been there either. But I sort of had to imagine they weren't there. And it's so beautiful, it's breathtaking.' (E2.402-414)

For others however, countryside experiences are enhanced by the company of others as Grant recalls:

'I think the question about favourite places, I'm afraid it's subjective to every person, you know. It's not just a case of the environment itself and the facilities there but it's the people you've been with there... It's not totally what the facilities are at all. It's a social thing as well. You've enjoyed being in the company or whatever at the time and you remember it for that. 'Cos I mean my favourite place... it's a big birch grove beside the river and they're not – the facilities there are a study room, a form, a picnic area with tables. And people swim in the river as well. I mean, I enjoy it. But I think I enjoy it most of all because I had good times there, you know, with friends.' (T2.504–7)

For many of the women in the Greenwich groups, the presence of company was an essential prerequisite before undertaking a visit to the countryside. Many felt frightened in 'empty' landscapes, felt frightened of sexual attack and in the case of Asian women, felt doubly at risk because of their gender and ethnicity. Similar expressions of the fear of being alone in the countryside were also expressed by a number of respondents in the groups conducted by the Qualitative Consultancy. In the light of these responses even people who want the 'freedom to roam' are unlikely to wish to be truly on their own, while for others the presence of companions and groups of friends is part of the countryside experience.

The Greenwich study suggests that even if the countryside is only visited infrequently, people seek out different physical settings and social contexts in which to enjoy themselves. For many working-class people and the Asian women, the agricultural countryside with its farms and fields, its villages and pubs, pick-your own farms and shops, woods and streams has immense appeal. By and large this is not the kind of countryside most statutory designations of the countryside for recreation seek to protect. Designations like National Parks and Country Parks may protect the wilderness areas that appeal to the middle-classes but the extent to which these designations also serve to provide access to the wider countryside is less clear. Equally, these protected areas may not promote the social context in which people can enjoy themselves either. Furthermore, for many people in the Greenwich groups, a visit to the countryside involved more than experiencing the sensual pleasures of being out in the country and away from the city. Most people also wanted to engage in the countryside as a 'better way of life' – experiences which might be characterized as the social meaning of the countryside.

The social meaning of the countryside

Williams (1975) shows how the country symbolizes a 'golden age' which has just been lost and he also illustrates how the 'country' is defined and experienced in a dialectical relationship with the 'city'. The country embodies all those qualities that are missing from the urban area and modern urban society. This ideal also permeates everyday life in many cultural forms.It finds expression in literature and art, in the concept of heritage and is reinforced through advertizing, in the newspapers and radio and TV (Burgess, 1990). The symbolic role of the countryside as a better way of life is also deeply embedded in the values of group members who contributed to these studies. Through the group discussions in the Greenwich study the social meaning of the countryside was revealed as one of the strongest reasons for visiting the countryside.

Country people were considered to have greater contact with, and appreciation of, nature and were expected to be more friendly and neighbourly, so that both family life and community life are regarded as more active and durable. Expressed in this way a visit to the countryside becomes a means of participating in that better way of life the city had displaced. Visits to farms, villages, pubs and pick your own farms allow people to engage briefly in country life even though they mock the pretence of 'urbs in rure' as the following exchange reveals.

Grant had lived in a fishing village in Shetland and he drew a clear distinction between different kinds of village life on the basis of its 'authenticity'.

> 'I think there's a big difference though between that type of village and villages in South-East England anyway, because they're not really villages... there's so many different people there and they work in advertising or they're accountants or in the centre of London, things like that. But they – it's a dormitory and they don't work locally, normally. Very few people do.'

> Tracy: 'They all commute don't they?'

> Malcolm: 'Yeah, they commute.'

> Grant: 'And it's a pretence of country life...'

> Malcolm: 'They go into the country and pretend they're countrymen. What are they living in? Converted oast houses... what they've converted themselves. They're not country people really. They kid themselves they are, but they're town people ain't they? (T3.1923–49).

People in all the groups acknowledged that this 'Golden Age' had passed, accepting that society itself had changed but, they all also acknowledged that visiting the countryside was a means of sharing in that better world. For many middle-class people the landscapes protected by the National Parks – the wilderness areas – represented the best examples of the countryside they desired to possess, but they *also* enjoyed visiting the wider countryside because of its social meaning.

That the wider countryside was changing in ways which statutory planning failed to control was also recognised by all three English groups. The growth of commuter settlements would ultimately lead to a point where there was no difference between town and country and people were quick to recognise the dilemma this posed. Gordon, and Marion for example said:

> Gordon: 'I think if you go and you find a place you like – 'I'd like to move there' – just by moving there you change the place because there's more interaction in the community and you bring other people and other people follow on, so you're changing the countryside.'

> Marion: 'That's right I just, I don't see there... being much left of it and then there won't be any comparison soon to make, you know, which is countryside.' (T3.2259–66).

Through the in-depth discussions of the Greenwich project it became clear just how deeply embedded in English culture is the social meaning of the countryside. Moreover, the groups expose why a supposedly unexceptional term like countryside invokes different meanings that are historically, socially and culturally constructed. The normative view that the countryside is best represented as those wilderness areas championed by the 'freedom to roam' movement fails to account for the popular appeal of the wider countryside. It also fails to take account of the strength of feeling that is expressed when the social structure of the working countryside becomes threatened by new residents whose livelihood is unrelated to the 'the countryside as a way of life'.

Perhaps the most important finding of the in-depth studies is that the term countryside is both culturally and socially defined. Critically however, although some aspects of the differing cultural idealizations of the countryside are class-related, people's *experience* of the countryside and their own personal circumstances give added meaning to the countryside. Often the countryside gains significance through the social occasion visits to the countryside represent. So, for example, many members of the Greenwich groups visited the countryside on occasions when they visited friends who lived in the countryside or when friends came to stay. Other people recalled visits which were memorable because of special events in their lives – on their honeymoon, just after bereavement, before their children were born or after their children had left home. In this way the countryside gains personal significance through 'incidents of incidence' and visits to the countryside are a means of keeping these experiences fresh and alive.

A final way in which these qualitative studies shed light on the social and cultural significance of the countryside is through their discussion of why people do not visit the countryside very often. For many people having access to a car was important and the absence of a car meant that some people did not visit the countryside as often as they would like. For others, visiting the countryside was a social occasion, often planned in advance and in discussion with friends and relatives. Visiting the countryside then became part of their wider social and leisure lives and not merely a question of knowing where to go or having the means of getting there. For a minority too, unhappy experiences and memories served to deter people from visiting the countryside.

The discussions held by the Qualitative Consultancy suggest that amongst young people in particular, the effort required to get to the country is not outweighed by the range of experiences they could find there. Many younger members regarded the countryside as somewhere essentially for adults. In this way enjoying the countryside is seen to reflect people's personal circumstances, stage in life cycle, and how they live out their social lives. Personal experience thus serves both to encourage and deter visits. As a result, although people's own circumstances may change and society itself may also change, the cultural and social significance of the countryside has enduring personal meaning and is one that is only poorly accounted for by class, education, income or car-ownership.

These in-depth studies suggest that much of the popular appeal of the countryside stems from the diversity of experiences both the farmed and settled countryside offers and from the rather more selective appeal of the wild and spectacular landscapes of the remote upland areas. They also suggest that most people value the wider countryside because of its symbolic role – the countryside as a better physical and social world. These intangible benefits of the countryside are widely-held and deeply felt but are often taken for granted and are difficult to express in answer to direct questions. Furthermore, attempts to measure the values of the countryside in terms of the number of visits made or people's willingness to pay for these trips assume that it is possible to quantify the depth of attachments people from all sections of society feel for the symbolic significance of different countrysides.

Given the undoubted attachment people have for the countryside, one of the major objectives of a national recreation policy might reasonably be expected to be an assurance that the wider countryside is planned and managed in ways that allow most people to share in this better way of life. But in England and Wales, where proprietorial rights convey on the owner a bundle of rights including the right of access, gaining access to the countryside pleasures people seek cannot be achieved without also challenging the attitudes and values of those private individuals and organizations who own the countryside. The growing tendency in modern society to use market mechanisms for gaining recreational access to the countryside (Centre for Leisure Research, 1986) impinges directly on the enjoyment of both organized users who favour non-market mechanisms for attaining access and of people who seek to enjoy the countryside in an informal way – the majority. How the public sector chooses to represent the interests of people who seek to enjoy the countryside in an informal and un-organized way is, therefore, of critical importance for the future recreational use of the countryside – especially the question of gaining access to and through it.

The 'Access Study'

Marion Shoard has forcefully argued (Shoard, 1987), that access to the countryside is not merely a question of private rights and the public good, it is also about differing 'ideologies' of the countryside. The findings of qualitative research support this contention because they show that people have differing ideas about which areas represent 'real' countryside and what kind of pleasures and activities are involved in enjoying the countryside.The *Access Study* (Countryside Commission, 1986) further shows that people differ in respect of the mechanisms which they believe are appropriate for gaining access to the countryside. This latter study concludes that the plurality of values expressed by the general public about countryside recreation is opposed by a more uniform set of attitudes to the recreational use of the countryside held by landowners and other 'resource controllers'. As a result some recreational interests have been able to gain access to the countryside resources they seek through a process of negotiation with landowners whilst others have not. This process of negotiation involves a matching of ideologies both in respect of accepting the appropriateness of particular recreational activities and the correctness of property rights as the legal basis for securing access to the countryside.

The *Access Study* arrives at this conclusion after a comprehensive investigation designed to find out why people who seek recreation in the countryside are either successful or frustrated in their attempts to exercise entry to the land and water resources of the countryside and to undertake particular activities on them. At the outset it makes an important distinction between access and accessibility.

Access refers to certain rights of approach, entry or use that are legally or conventionally defined, whereas accessibility refers to the extent to which these rights can be exercised in particular places, at particular times and by particular people. This distinction serves to emphasize that in England and Wales the law does not recognise public access as a legal right, as it does, for example, in many Scandinavian countries through the legal right of 'Allemansratten'. All land in England and Wales is owned by someone and ownership conveys with it the right to control access. Even common land is owned by a Lord of the Manor and the public currently have a legal right of access to only one fifth of all common land. In consequence, the public enjoy only restricted or permissive access even to land that is nominally in 'public' ownership. The study illustrates too, that even where rights of access are available, these are the product of a transaction entered into between the landowner – including local authorities, and those who seek access. Such transactions produce varying degrees of access. Often local by-laws restrict use to some users and not others and by offering permissive rights rather than statutory rights, the security of access they result in differs too.

One of the important contributions the *Access Study* makes is to demonstrate that all such transactions reflect both differing concepts of 'appropriate recreation' and differing views about the role proprietorial rights play as the legal basis for securing access to the countryside. Viewed in this way, the extent to which the countryside is accessible to different people reflects not only their own material circumstances and where they live, but also the differing attitudes and values of those people and groups in society who control access to the countryside – both private and public. As a result some groups with an interest in the recreational use of the countryside, like Naturalists' Trusts, Mountaineering and Angling Groups have been able to secure access to areas for their recreational activities, whilst others, like motor sports and several water sports, have not been able to press their claims. Critical too, in the light of the qualitative studies which show that much of people's enjoyment is gained by visiting a wide variety of physical and social settings in the farmed and settled countryside, is the extent to which informal as well as organized recreational interests are taken into account in access negotiations.

At the outset of the *Access Study*, a clear distinction was made between 'informal recreationists' who engage in a wide range of activities in the countryside but in a spontaneous and unorganized way, and people who belong to organizations and groups. By examining the extent to which these respective constituencies participate in the process of planning and allocating recreational provision, the study focuses attention on the various strategies used by the public and private sectors to secure access to the countryside. People who are 'informal recreationsists' generally only participate in the planning and allocation of recreational resources indirectly whereas organized groups have more direct involvement.

The main way in which local authorities and national agencies concerned with recreation have attempted to take account of demands for informal recreation is by having recourse to 'standards of open space provision' (see Chapter 2). Such standards have played a prominent role in provision of open space in the urban area but, no comparable standards exist for countryside recreation or outdoor sports which take place beyond the urban area. Nevertheless, in general recognition of the fact that the market is not a good allocator of informal recreational requirements, the public sector has intervened in provision. Local authorities have a statutory obligation to maintain a Rights of Way network and authorities have purchased land for use as Public Open Space. However the variable investment made by differing local authorities in open space provision and their failure to maintain the Rights of Way network, means that public provision for countryside recreation is itself uneven and of variable quality. Moreover, prevailing attitudes amongst providers to 'appropriate use' may favour some informal, 'un-organised' interests and not others – that is walking and horseriding rather than camping, trail-bike or motor cycling and fishing and sailing rather than motor-boating or water skiing (Sports Council, 1990b).

By contrast many environmental and sports groups, participate directly in decision-making – by consultation, representation, and lobbying (Lowe and Goyder, 1983). In this way public agencies are kept informed of the demands of organized groups even in those circumstances where the market is a poor allocator of their claims. The *Access Study* demonstrates how some organized groups have been successful in pressing their claims for access through direct processes of consultation.

It is much more difficult for public agencies to act on behalf of the interests of informal recreation unless these agencies decide to research what people want. In theory, the normative standards set by planners or policy makers are designed to represent the requirements of informal recreationists and people who enjoy unorganised sports. But as earlier chapters have shown, these standards may not adequately reflect what people want, especially under circumstances of changing demand, and when there is no common agreement about what form standards of provision for countryside recreation might take, or a well-recognized professional institution to determine such standards, the attitudes and values of individual providers are likely to have a strong influence on the kind of provision made. In these circumstances the interests of informal recreation are unlikely to be served very effectively unless the public sector chooses deliberately to research and pursue them.

One of the main objectives of the *Access Study* was to examine the access requirements of both informal recreationists and organised groups and to explore how their requirements differed from those of resource controllers, including those public agencies with a responsibility for recreation. A questionnaire survey was undertaken in areas where actual and potential demand for access might be expected to be high – that is around major cities and amongst households which did not have access to a car. 1,600 interviews were used in their analysis. The views of organised recreationists and sports groups were assessed using a semi- structured interview conducted with representatives of a number of national and local groups. A mixed-mode approach was adopted for assessing the attitudes of resource controllers. The views of private landowners, tenants and managers were sought in a farm interview survey in each of the four study tracts – Snowdon-Lleyn,

Pennines-Peak, East Midlands and East Dorset. Interviews were also conducted with representatives from national and regional public bodies which own and manage land or water. Organizations and agencies such as the Country Landowners' Association, Department of the Environment, National Farmers' Union etc.

Representatives of conservation and amenity groups were also interviewed on the grounds that these organisations have recently emerged as a growing influence on the use of the countryside and access to it (Lowe and Goyder, 1983). Representatives from organisations such as the National Trust, Council for the Protection of Rural England and the Open Spaces Society were amongst those who were interviewed to assess their policies, attitudes and concerns about access to the countryside. Members of county and local authorities involved in major planning initiatives such as Access Agreements were also interviewed, both with respect to these agreements and in relation to the condition and management of public rights of way and their attitudes to the seeming conflict between nature conservation and recreation. Selected interviews were also held with members of local authorities, voluntary bodies and trusts who were involved in specific countryside management schemes and access initiatives.

The findings of the *Access Study* are summarized in the following sections.

Attitudes amongst recreationists

The study highlights the diversity of attitudes to the recreational use of the countryside held by recreationists. In particular, organised groups differ in respect of the strategies they use to press their access claims to the countryside (exclusionary, co-operative or principle) and to the access mechanisms they employ to secure these claims (non-market and market). The study like Lowe and Goyder (1983) draws a distinction between 'interest' and 'principle' groups. The former are defined as appointed representatives for a particular part of the community which expresses a specific interest or set of interests such as those of riders, canoeists etc. Principle groups do not pursue sectional interests but rather seek to defend or promote commonly held values such as the 'freedom to roam' or 'public rights' over water and land. In each case however, as Pepper has suggested, both groups often expound ecocentric beliefs and attempt to advance their claims by seeking to preserve land for the 'benefit of nature and mankind'.

Table 4.3: Access strategies
Source: Countryside Commission, 1984

Access Mechanisms	Approaches		
	Exclusionary	Cooperative	Participatory
Non-market			
de facto	mountaineers	canoeists	Ramblers' Association
legal/statutory	local ramblers	local ramblers	Ramblers' Association
		Trail Riders Federation	Byways and Bridleways
		British Horse Society	Trust
		British Canoe Union	Open Spaces Society
Market			
private rights	anglers		
	(conservationists)		
permission	riding schools	British Canoe Union	
	British Mountaineering		
	Club		

The most common strategies pursued by interest and principle groups are illustrated in Table 4.3. Amongst interest groups, exclusionary approaches seek to impose restrictive definitions of 'legitimate' activities and claims for access, whilst co-operative approaches seek to share a particular resource with existing interests. This latter approach is often adopted by new recreational interests seeking access to the countryside. In both cases either non-market or market mechanisms may be used as the basis for securing access. Participatory approaches used by principle groups are more altruistic and are pursued in the belief that the wider public will be beneficiaries. In this case, principle groups are often unwilling to use market mechanisms as the basis for access negotiations.

The *Access Study* emphasizes that this typology is indicative only of a wide range of possible strategies. It also illustrates other difficulties; for example, local strategies may not always coincide with national policies, different strategies may be used within the same sport and some conservationists, like some recreationists, seek to secure exclusive use for their members. In both these latter cases questions of social equity arise especially when such groups seek to extend their access requirements into those areas which are already popular destinations for informal recreationists – areas like the Peak District for example with a long-tradition of de facto access and the numerous canals, estuaries and urban-fringe areas that have an equally long tradition of established but non-conforming users.

The attitudes of 'resource controllers'

The diversity of attitudes to the countryside and its appropriate uses identified amongst people who use and wish to use the countryside for recreation, contrasts with the more homogeneous set of core values held by landowners and resource controllers. Amongst farmers there was a general reluctance to extend existing access arrangements and in some cases outright hostility to them – even to the extent of an unwillingness to negotiate with organized groups. Other statutory landowning organisations exhibited ambivalent attitudes towards the issue of extending access, although in practice, how the resource was managed rather than ownership influenced attitudes to extending public access. For example, at a time when the financial future of the farming industry is less secure than in the recent past, the NFU expressed qualified support for extending access agreements as long as some financial compensation was paid to the landowner. Likewise, land-owners who strongly supported a business approach to managing their farm as an economic enterprise rather than as a 'way-of-life', were more sympathetic to extending public access. In both cases however, new access arrangements would be secured only as part of a financial transaction.

Effectively this market approach is a reversal of the 'polluter-pays' principle which has gained ground within the EC as a means of regulating private and public rights in other spheres of environmental policy. Were such market approaches to be extended into the realm of countryside access, then individuals and charitable organisations would clearly be at a disadvantage in such negotiations. In addition, the changing political context in which public utilities and other statutory organisations such as Water Authorities, Electricity Boards, The Railway Board and the Forestry Commission have been privatized or are being urged by central government to review opportunities for privatisation, also means that participatory access approaches are seldom pursued. Because land subject to access arrangements with different user groups might reduce the market value of land, new access arrangements are unlikely to be entertained and permissive access rights are vulnerable because they can be terminated quickly. In this way, substantial tracts of the countryside, coast and waterways which are nominally in the public domain are effectively 'closed to the public' unless enabling legislation provides for public access. The recent history of water privatization in England and Wales is a case in point. Only after concerted lobbying by the Countryside Commission and other amenity groups were precautionary clauses included in national legislation. As a result conservation organizations have first refusal in the event that Water Authority holdings subject to conservation designation are offered for sale on the open market.

The study also reveals how discrepancies arise between the attitudes of national resource controllers and the views of their members. For example in interviews with the researchers, the National Farmers Union chose to characterise the issue of access to rural land in terms of the 'alien urban hordes' over-running the rural area. By contrast, the survey of farmers had shown that most farmers regard local residents and new-comers to the area as the main groups causing problems related to access. In these circumstances only local policies are likely to address these access problems and not some generally applied national policy.

The tendency for national resource controllers to support the status-quo rather than to reflect the changing demands and expectations of all recreationists is also apparent in the statutory planning system. It is basically slow to respond to changes in demand although even amongst public authorities, the endeavours and commitment of individual officers and the views of elected members can lead to differing approaches to access. The *Access Study* cites the differing approaches to access pursued by certain Naturalists' and Wildlife Trusts in collaboration with public authorities and national agencies. For example it notes the restrictive nature of access agreements in Snowdonia when compared with those policies pursued in the Peak District. The study also reveals differences too in the way public authorities exercise their powers to intervene in securing access to the countryside for different activities. For example, horse-riders are more acceptable than motor cyclists and anglers are more acceptable than pleasure boaters. In practice the burden of evidence suggests that public authorities remain predictably resistant to the claims of particular activities. Elson et al. (1986a and b) in their study of motor sports illustrate convincingly how a long established recreational use of the countryside – motor sports, with a tradition of countryside use at least as long as the Ramblers, has failed to gain legitimacy through the planning system. In part this failure is a reflection of the unwillingness of organisers of motor sports to adopt a politically-active approach, but it also reflects the growing influence of *'localism'* and the influence of local rate-payers who define the countryside in terms of the aesthetic tradition and in terms of peace and quiet. As a result, some activities and users are effectively excluded from gaining access to the countryside even in areas where they have a long tradition of permissive use.

Overall, it is this question of legitimacy which underpins the access issue. Fundamentally 'the battle for access is as much concerned with values as it is with access mechanisms' (p.53 Access Study.) There is mounting evidence to suggest that newly emerging recreational activities, including a wide variety of water sports which demand access to the water, and the growth in 'unacceptable' activities such as motors sports, trail bikes and mountain bikes are unlikely to gain access to the territory they require unless the public sector makes a deliberate attempt to promote and accommodate them. Moreover, it is apparent that the growth in unorganised recreation and sports is far greater than the growth in membership of established organizations. The *Access Study* quotes figures for The British Canoe Union's estimate of canoeists of about 100,000, although the membership of the Union is at present only 11,000. Likewise, the paid up membership of the Ramblers' Association stands at 79,000 but there is widespread consensus that up to 10 million people go regularly for a long walk of 2 miles or more at a weekend. In practice membership numbers fail to reflect the size of the constituency which enjoys the countryside in an informal way. Moreover, organisations which purport to represent both their members and the sport in general, run the risk of curtailing permissive access by casual users if they pursue exclusive use for members only. Above all, countryside recreation is enjoyed because of its informality – often because it is a social occasion, sometimes as a means of seeking spiritual renewal, self-awareness and physical prowess but for the majority often as a means of engaging in the 'better way of life' the countryside represents. To organize countryside recreation is to deny those central values which are axiomatic to its enjoyment and to rely on negotiated access mechanisms is to deny that permissible free access would provide most people with the pleasures they seek.

In the final analysis the *Access Study* concludes that very few organisations pursue non-exclusive, public rights for multi-purpose uses. Under these circumstances, the onus on public authorities to act in the interest of the activity, rather than to respond to particular user organizations, is an important and growing one. But crucially too, at a time of genuine uncertainty about the relationship between increasing leisure time and potential growth in countryside recreation is the need to recognize that the countryside is enjoyed in a wide diversity of ways by people from all parts of the social spectrum. As long as countryside recreation is defined as the enjoyment of peace and quiet and access to countryside areas is defined as a positional good to be negotiated and determined by proprietorial interests, some groups and users in society will continue to benefit and others will not. For example organized groups with resources and a matching ideology are likely to benefit from this system but others who refuse to become organized and who are unwilling to pay for access, will not. Whether or not this dominant ideology is likely to be challenged at a time when both the attitudes of farmers and the public are changing, is a question explored in Chapter 8.

Conclusion

Public enjoyment of the countryside in England and Wales, whether involving visits to specific sites or to the wider countryside, is underpinned by a complex system of negotiated access rights. That most people who use the countryside for informal recreation and outdoor activities do so in ignorance of these transactions is in part a measure of the complexity which surrounds property rights in the first place. In part it is also a measure of the successful intervention by public agencies and authorities in the inter-war period to secure, more or less enduring rights of access to public open spaces in the countryside and to the extensive Rights of Way network. In Shoard's view however, it is in large measure a reflection of how readily people have become inured to the powers of a landowning elite. The studies reviewed here provide some support for her view.

Qualitative studies reveal that amongst the public, views differ about what countryside means, what constitutes appropriate use of the countryside and what mechanisms can be used to secure access to the countryside. For these reasons the prospects for increased conflicts among recreationists themselves and between recreationists, conservationists and environmentalists are likely to prove just as contentious as those between landowner and the public. Significant for the manner in which these conflicts might be resolved however, is the growing tendency detected in the *Access Study*, to treat the countryside as a positional good by new residents, organized groups with a recreational interest in the countryside, environmentalists, and landowners. Coupled with financial constraints on public authorities, this tendency is likely to mean that some groups of recreationsists will succeed in pressing their claims to access both because their attitudes and values support the ideology of the countryside aesthetic and the correctness of market mechanisms for gaining access. Other uses which challenge this ideology and the acceptance of market mechanisms as the only means of securing access to the countryside, are unlikely to be successful in advancing their claims.

The Countryside Commission's response to new demands for widening access to the countryside as revealed through their programme of action (Countryside Commission, 1987a), is to strengthen *existing* statutory mechanisms such as compliance with the Rights of Way legislation, better use of Access and Management Agreements and the pursuit of partnership initiatives with the private and voluntary sectors. None of these activities challenge the dominant ideology of the countryside aesthetic or its social and cultural basis in proprietorial rights. So for example, the Rights of Way Act 1990 clarifies the position about how the costs for maintaining existing rights of way can be assigned and recovered but, unless local authorities choose to use these new powers, no improvements in access will result. Likewise the failure of the Common Land Forum to secure wider public access to moorlands managed for game, reflects the continued dominance of landed interests (Countryside Commission, 1986) in spite of evidence that disturbance to sheep and game by walkers is minimal (Sidaway, 1990).

Shoard's solution to this conflict of values is to re-write the statute books in favour of a new right of access whereby every one has the right to pass over another's land. Coupled with a land tax which penalizes landowners who do not manage their land in accordance with national, regional and local plans and which benefits those who do, Shoard's vision is of a landscape managed to create an *agreed* land-use outcome. In other words she envisages a countryside in which recreation, access and conservation interests are treated on a par with productive interests like farming and forestry. This radical solution challenges the power which landowners wield to manage their own land as they feel fit. It also assumes that legalizing access and managing the countryside will reconcile conflicts among recreationists and between recreationists and other land users – land reform will challenge the dominance of the 'countryside aesthetic' and management plans will provide the means of securing agreement.

Wresting the bundle of rights that landownership confers from those who own them is likely to require nothing less than a social revolution and identifying and implementing agreed management plans would also prove difficult given the evidence presented here about the plurality of values held by the public. Hence in the absence of a new Access Charter, it is pertinent to examine the efficacy of existing recreation policies for securing access to the range of environments and experiences qualitative studies reveal most people seek. The book now turns to a critical examination of two specific policies which have dominated public sector involvement in countryside recreation, namely site-based policies of provision based on Country Parks and Regional Parks, and policies designed to promote the recreational use of the countryside by public transport. Both are policies which have been justified on the grounds that they are socially motivated, and both have been pursued in the interests of unorganized, informal recreation. But, as Chapters 5 and 6 will show, these policies are also predicated on a number of assumptions about why and how people enjoy the countryside.

5

Site-based policies and countryside recreation
....

Introduction

After 1968 when the responsibilities for national policies for countryside recreation were given to the Countryside Commission, the main
way in which the public sector intervened in countryside recreation
was through the pursuit of a site-based policy. Through this policy,
the provision of recreation facilities became concentrated on sites designated as Country Parks and a few Regional Parks, and after 1974,
when the Commission gave priority to provision in the urban fringe,
the thrust of the Commission's recreation policy was directed to these
locations. The rationale for pursuing this site-based policy has always
been two-fold; first, to contain where recreation demand falls in the
countryside and second to provide attractive recreational opportunities close to where demand lies. As earlier chapters have shown this
duality arises partly from the Commission's own remit for conservation and recreation and partly from the dominant attitudes amongst
other public authorities which regarded popular countryside recreation as a problem to be managed rather than an opportunity for building a better society. The purpose of this chapter is to examine how
successful this locational policy has been in terms of both containing
where demand falls on the countryside and extending the range of
recreational opportunities available in the countryside – especially to
urban residents who do not have access to a car.

The rationale for site-based policies

The rising popular demand for countryside recreation experienced
throughout the 1960s brought responses from both the private and
public sector. In some respects the private sector was quicker to

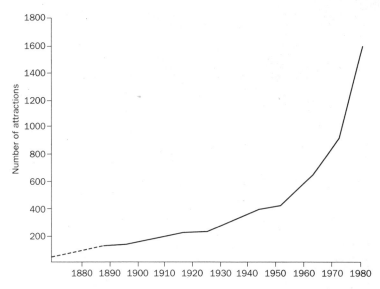

Figure 5.1: Growth in number of a sample of attractions in England
Source: Sports Council, 1983

respond to this growth in demand than the various public authorities. New facilities were opened up in the countryside many of them developed by the private sector and several were located in the countryside around towns rather than in the urban area (Figure 5.1 and Table 5.1). Disused gravel pits were converted for water sports, stately homes were opened up to the public, often for the first time, and safari parks, gardens and zoos were just some of the new attractions developed. By 1972, 72% of the adult population of south-east England (excluding the GLC) had made at least one visit during the year to a stately home, zoo, attractive village or wildlife park and over 35% had made more than five of these visits during the year. In the case of Londoners, participation by the adult population in informal recreation trips of this kind proved to be more popular than any other out of home activity, with the exception of social drinking (GLC, 1975–6). There was thus both a growing demand for countryside recreation and a growing momentum to provide new recreational facilities in the countryside. The arguments used in the public sector to advance a site-based approach to provision located in the urban fringe however, were not solely designed to provide new opportunities which would meet market demand. Indeed, if this were the case there would be little justification for advocating public sector involvement. Rather, as Elson (1972) has shown, several arguments were advanced.

Table 5.1: Growth in number of a sample of attractions in England (by percentage of those responding to an English Tourist Board Survey)
Source: Sports Council, 1983

Period first opened to public	Historic buildings %	Gardens %	Museums & Art Galleries %	Wildlife attractions %	Others %	All %
1980	2	2	3	1	4	3
1970–1979	34	43	41	47	62	42
1960–1969	17	23	16	31	15	17
1950–1959	18	12	8	7	6	11
1940–1949	5	4	2	1	2	3
1930–1939	5	4	5	4	3	5
1920–1929	4	6	7	2	4	5
1910–1919	1	–	2	–	–	1
1900–1909	2	3	4	–	1	2
1890–1899	1	–	2	2	–	2
1880–1889	1	–	3	1	1	2
Pre 1880	10	3	7	4	2	7
	100	100	100	100	100	100
No. of attractions	522	111	730	98	254	1,715

In his review of the *Leisure Use of Green Belts and Urban Fringes*, Elson points to several reasons used to justify locating recreation in the urban-fringe. These are:

* because the urban fringe is close to where demand is greatest provision located in the fringe will be well used and cost-effective because journeys will be shorter;

* because the urban fringe is more accessible by public transport than the deeper countryside, people who do not own a car can gain access to it;

* by locating provision in the urban fringe, some visitors will be deflected from visiting sites elsewhere in the more distant countryside. As a result quiet areas and some vulnerable sites may be better protected;

* derelict or under-used land in the urban-fringe can be brought into beneficial use, including recreational use.

Several assumptions underpin these arguments although two are of critical importance to cultural and social aspects of provision. First, it is assumed that by altering supply, demand can be intercepted and redistributed. In other words, it is assumed that new provision in sites managed specially for recreation will prove to be attractive and will appeal to all those who seek countryside recreation. Second, it is assumed that provision located in the urban fringe is accessible to people who do not have access to a car and to people who live in inner city areas remote from where provision is located. In the discussion which follows, a number of empirical studies are used to test the validity of these assumptions.

Site-based policies as a means of influencing where demand falls

Under the the widened remit accorded to the Countryside Commission in the 1968 Act, the Countryside Commission was given new powers to grant-aid both public and private sectors for developing and managing new recreation facilities called Country Parks. These latter had been proposed in the White Paper, '*Leisure and the Countryside*' (1966). From the outset however, no objective standards of provision were set for Country Parks or for their functions and facilities. The Commission's view of a Country Park as 'an area of land, normally more than 25 acres in extent, with basic facilities for the public to enjoy informal open air recreation' (Countryside Commission, 1974) indicates little about the role these parks were expected to play. Their *Advice Notes* (1974) on Country Parks are cast in equally general terms and provide little guidance about the balance between conservation and recreation, between education and enjoyment, or between 'rural' sports such as riding and fishing and other sports such as pleasure boating or motor sports. There is equal uncertainty about the extent to which provision might be regarded as a social service. Nevertheless, by giving priority to provision located in urban-fringe areas, new opportunities were assumed to be accessible to urban residents who did not own cars. In Scotland the Country Parks were regarded as contributing to a parkland system that embraced the whole of Scotland (Countryside Commission for Scotland, 1974) but their functions too were described only in general terms:

* To provide within a parkland system for Scotland a variety of convenient areas in each of which people can enjoy a wide range of open air leisure pursuits, both passive and active, with or without charge, in pleasant rural surroundings;

* To ease pressure of public use on vulnerable scenic and wildlife areas and high quality farmland and woodland and thereby reduce risk of damage to them;

95

Table 5.2: Suggestions for facilities for outdoor recreation based on a survey of householders
Source: Duffield and Owen, 1971

Central Scotland: Provision of facilities for outdoor recreation

Facility	General	Country Parks
	(percentage of all choices)	
Children's amusements	12.4	15.2
Indoor games	11.1	3.1
Swimming pool	10.3	5.1
Tennis	6.9	5.7
Football	6.6	4.7
Golf	5.2	8.2
Parks	4.4	0.7
Bowls (outdoor)	4.4	2.2
Sports (stadium)	3.2	2.3
Youth hostels	3.0	0.6
Boating	2.6	8.9
Gardens	2.3	5.6
Walks	2.0	2.7
Ice rink	1.7	0.4
Sports (coach)	1.6	0.6
Fishing	1.6	1.6
Riding	1.3	1.8
Skiing	1.2	0.7
Cafe/hotel	1.2	4.5
Nature reserves	1.0	1.8

※ To help towards a better understanding of the need for conservation through a planned and controlled use of parts of the countryside for leisure pursuits and by including, where applicable, an interpretive function for the town dweller to appreciate countryside and the point of view of the countryman.

This essentially multi-functional role found some acceptance amongst householders in Central Scotland, as Duffield and Owen's study (1971) reveals. In this survey people were asked about their suggestions for facilities for outdoor recreation in general and in Country Parks in particular. More than 140 different facilities were mentioned in their replies, many of them the kinds of facilities that might be found in urban parks. Only 4% mentioned the 'natural elements' of the countryside that people planning the parks thought essential (see Table 5.2). Clearly at this early date in the history of Country Parks, the concept of a Country Park had not made much impact on public thinking and planners remained unsure about the influence public preferences and demand should have on the type of provision Country Parks might offer. This uncertainty about the extent to which park provision might be guided by need rather than normative

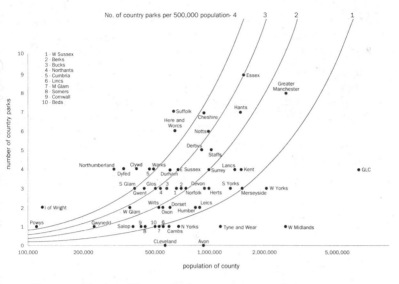

Figure 5.2: Number of Country Parks per 500,000 population.
Source: Groome and Tarrant, 1984

expectations of professionals or the 'standards of provision' favoured by planners, resulted in a pattern of provision that was guided at most by expressed demand and principally, as Slee (1982) has suggested, by the momentum generated by grant-aid itself.

Several studies have provided an account of the ways in which Country Park policy emerged, for example Zetter, (1971) Slee, (1982), and Groome and Tarrant, (1984). All emphasize that little serious attempt has been made to determine whether or not the parks provide the kinds of recreational experiences most people seek. Groome and Tarrant's analysis (1984), which relates park provision for 1982 to population as a crude indication of public demand illustrates just how poor this relationship is (Figure 5.2). In practice, those authorities which already had proposals in the pipeline at the time when the new grants were announced, quickly took advantage of them. Cheshire was amongst the first to respond with its proposal for the Wirral Way, a linear park based around a disused railway, and Derbyshire and Lancashire followed close behind. By 1971 several authorities had taken initiatives to designate Country Parks and to propose Country Park status for several existing public open spaces. In the eighteen months after the Act came into force 50 applications for Country Parks had been made in the South East region alone (Standing Conference on London and South East Regional Planning, 1979). By 1976 some

97

130 such parks had been designated in England and Wales as a whole, although the pattern of provision was diffuse and regionally variable (Figure 5.6).

During the mid-seventies the Countryside Commission came to place increasing importance on the need for recreation provision in the urban fringe. Initially, the 1968 Act had required relevant authorities to have regard to the location of Country Parks in relation to an urban or built up area, and to the availability and adequacy of existing facilities for the enjoyment of countryside by the public (Section 6). After the Local Government Act of 1972 when financial assistance for countryside works was operated through the rate-support grant to Local Authorities, the Commission gave urban-fringe areas priority for grant aid. Groome and Tarrant (1984) suggest that this spatial priority was reflected in designations after 1974 but again large disparities in provision still remained. For example, among the metropolitan authorities at this time only Manchester with its eight Country Parks and South Yorkshire with three parks had more than one park/ 500,000 population. Around London some 17 Country Parks had been designated by 1978 in the Green Belt but there were no Country Parks in the Berkshire green belt and neither Surrey nor Kent had established Country Parks under their own management (Ferguson and Munton, 1979).

New opportunities or duplication of provision?

In practice many of the sites designated as Country Parks were already in some form of public ownership before they acquired Country Park status. Curry (1985) suggests that 60% of the land area designated between 1968 and 1974 fell in this category. Several sites around London like Trent Park were Public Open Spaces acquired under the Green Belt and Home Counties Act of 1938 and others, like many of the Surrey commons, such as Frensham Common, had been acquired by county authorities under independent Acts of Parliament initiated at an earlier date. Only when Country Park provision was linked to the up-grading of derelict land such as wet gravel pits or disused railway lines were new recreational resources added to the existing supply of countryside sites. Even then, there is little evidence to suggest that detailed considerations of accessibility were taken into account in decisions to establish one site rather than another, especially during a period when the public transport network was being cut back. Moreover, because the Countryside Commission could only respond to requests for grant support from local authorities rather than initiate

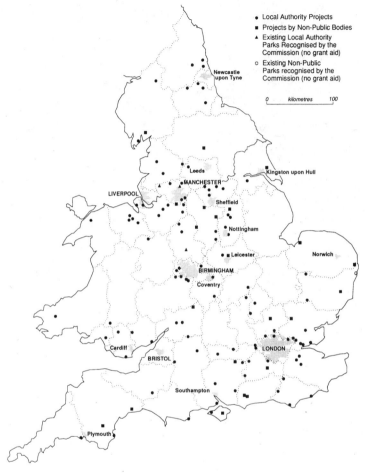

Figure 5.3: Country Parks, 1976
Source: Countryside Commission,1976

new proposals themselves, provision remained spatially uneven around most major urban centres and reflected the enthusiasm of particular authorities and officers rather than overall considerations of demand and supply. Ferguson and Munton's 1979 study of recreation provision in the London Green belt shows how the proposal for Horton Country Park in Surrey took little account of spatial inequalities in supply elsewhere in the Green Belt and merely served to reinforce a pattern of provision inherited from the inter-war period.

99

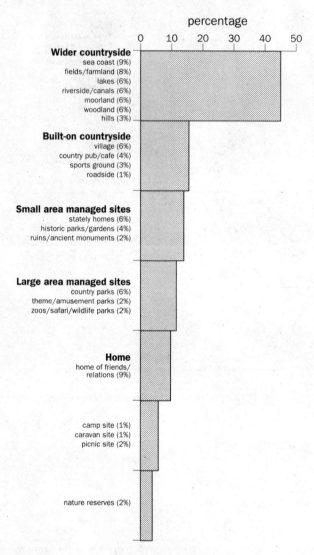

Figure 5.4: Countryside recreation trips and their destinations
Source: Countryside Commission, 1984

The priority given to urban fringe areas has undoubtedly assisted local authorities in maintaining a supply of recreational sites close to the urban edge which otherwise might have fallen prey to development, agricultural improvement or forestry. But the extent to which they provided genuinely new recreational opportunities is debatable. The absence of any detailed recreational surveys before the early 1970s, also means that it is difficult to guage what impact this site policy had on redistributing where demand fell in the countryside. Nevertheless, Fitton's analysis of the 1977 national recreation surveys gives some indication of the relative importance of different countryside facilities. His analysis shows that Country Parks which comprised 0.13%, just over one thousandth, of the total land surface of England and Wales were the main destination of 4.2% of trips although just over a third of all countryside trips were to sites managed specifically for recreation. This position had not changed significantly by 1984 as Figure 5.4 shows. Such figures suggest that the un-managed country-side provides attractive destinations for most people rather than sites specifically managed for recreation and even then it is difficult to determine what role Country Park destinations located in the urban fringe play in this overall pattern of trip behaviour.

Elson's analysis of the trip characteristics of visitors to 31 sites in the countryside of South East England (Countryside Commission, 1979) lends general support to Fitton's findings. By classifying sites in a qualitative way on the basis of location in relation to population centres, size (area and numbers of visitors), the range of facilities provided and the type and rarity of natural environment, the 31 sites used in the SIRSEE study were divided into six groups. These groups formed the basis for an examination of the association between site-type and trip characteristics (Figure 5.5a and 5.5b). Trip distances to urban fringe sites were shorter than distances recorded to other sites with 75% being under 20 kilometres, although the length of time people stayed at these sites was longer than those recorded for visits to villages and small informal picnic sites. Longer trips and visits were recorded to coastal sites and historic properties. Whether these differences relate to distances away from the home or to the kinds of environments and facilities afforded at different sites could not be determined from this kind of analysis. The provision of play facilities for children had an influence on the proportion of groups which included children, for example 57% at historic properties which provided play facilities compared with 42% at picnic sites.

The proportions of visitors in different socio-economic groups also differed by site with the large informal countryside sites attracting the highest proportion of people in managerial and professional

101

Site type by trip distance – South East site study 1973

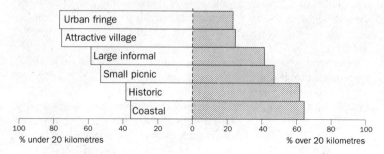

Figure 5.5a: Site type by trip distance – South East site study 1973
Source: Elson, 1979

Site type by length of stay – South East site study 1973

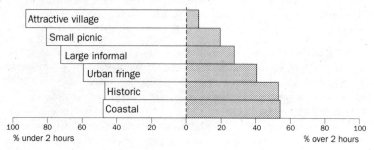

Figure 5.5b: Site type by length of stay – South East site study 1973
Source: Elson, 1979

occupations. Urban fringe sites and those sites which offered a range of facilities, were visited more regularly than other destinations. On the basis of this analysis and a careful appraisal of several other regional recreational surveys Elson concludes that:

> 'whilst distance-decay functions effectively summarize relationships between population distribution and sites at a high level of generality they subsume such factors as inter-site variations, the reduction in knowledge by distance from an individual's home, and less easily measurable mea-surable factors surrounding individual's choices within the environment of recreation opportunity.' (Elson, 1979, para.3.33, p.60)

Country Parks were represented in four of the six site-types used in

Elson's analysis but his analysis did not suggest that they acted as distinctive recreational attractions even when analyzed by location.

Other studies lend support to his conclusions. For example a detailed study of one of the largest Country Parks, Cannock Chase located in the countryside outside Stafford in the West Midlands, revealed that this park 'functioned' as a set of discrete sites, each with their own catchment area and each perceived slightly differently in terms of the environments and facilities they offered (Countryside Commission, 1984). The sites with the most facilities proved to be most popular within the park. They also attracted the largest number of first time visitors who themselves were undertaking a visit to the wider countryside and not to the park *per se*. In this sense the park had not achieved a separate identity but people's *experiences* of particular sites within it, had contributed to their own separate evaluations of what particular locations offered.

Questions which asked about changes peoples would like to see in the Chase brought contradictory responses. 60% wanted substantial changes in visitor facilities and 21% wanted to see further restrictions on visitor access. The consultants concluded that the Park

> 'must cater both for a mass of visitors who want comfort and convenience on their trip to the countryside, and for a substantial minority who resent any change that will detract from their sense of escaping from the town and from the mass of the population when they come to the Chase.'
> (Countryside Commission 1982, p.39).

The duality this study revealed about the recreational role Country Parks are expected to play by people who visit them, suggests that there is a substantial gap between what providers think people should enjoy when out in the countryside and what visitors themselves enjoy.

Other studies too suggest that Country Parks have not achieved a distinctive identity and that they may not provide the range of opportunities and experiences people seek when they visit the countryside. So for example, studies reported by the Countryside Commission (1988) reveal that although 58% of the population claimed to have heard of Country Parks, only 26% named a specific Country Park correctly and 13% named a site thinking it was a Country Park. Since national surveys reveal that most countryside visiting takes place to the wider countryside rather than to specific sites managed for recreation, this low level of knowledge is only to be expected. Moreover, since only very limited attempts have been made to promote Country Parks through the dissemination of literature, sign posting or through the use of local press and radio facilities, it is not surprising to find that they lack a clear identity and figure infrequently in the responses generated by household surveys.

In part, this failure to promote Country Parks is a reflection of the Commission's twin responsibilities for both conservation and recreation and from the wording of the 1968 Act which gives the Commission powers to *facilitate* outdoor recreation but not to promote it. Creating new provision is itself a form of promotion but, the absence of a positive promotion policy also reflects the reluctance of other public authorities to actively encourage countryside recreation. Amongst the Commission's partners in provision, the dominant attitude towards recreation always regarded popular countryside recreation as a problem and a threat. By exercising these attitudes through a site-based policy, provision came to *duplicate* rather than extend recreational opportunities. By doing so, the public sector served to protect the interests of private landowners and a particular ideology of the countryside and its appropriate recreational use.

New policies for Country Parks outlined in the Commission's recent policy statement show that these attitudes still prevail:

> 'Country parks and other major sites can take large numbers of visitors who want a convenient place in which to relax within easy reach of major centre of demand. This relieves the pressure of visitors on the surrounding countryside.' (p.21 CCP 234, 1987)

Interestingly too, these new policies aim to develop and manage parks as venues for a range of sporting activities, especially water-based ones.

> 'But sites must be large enough and managed so that sports activities do not interfere with more casual use and the quiet enjoyment of the countryside.'

The inference here is that when questions of competing uses arise, the nineteenth century aesthetic ideal of the countryside is to prevail rather than the interests of particular activities or people the site can best serve.

In essence, the site-based approach to provision is predicated on the assumption that quiet enjoyment and only this form of enjoyment is what most people seek when out in the countryside, even though numerous studies suggest that the majority of users enjoy engaging in a range of activities. At Cannock Chase for example less than a quarter of visitors said that they came because of the particular aesthetic, natural or environmental qualities, many more said they came because it was safe for the children or for generally social reasons largely unconnected with the distinctive opportunities that the Chase landscape has to offer.

Other in-depth studies of people's attitudes to the enjoyment of the countryside also emphasise the social orientation of visits (see Chapter 4). The peace and quiet of the countryside which most Country Parks seek to conserve has wide appeal but it is only one of many ways of enjoying the countryside. Moreover, the tendency of many Country Parks to pursue conservation objectives rather than recreational ones serves to favour some forms of countryside enjoyment rather than others. Passive enjoyment of the countryside rather than a more active participation in a range of activities is favoured and solitary activities are favoured rather than social occasions and gatherings like, fairs, shows, rallies or merely crowds of friends and relatives. This 'culture of provision' is likely to have social consequences if through lack of opportunity Country Parks do not provide the range of pleasurable experiences most people seek. Conversely, a coincidence of cultural preferences between providers and people who visit the countryside most frequently, may help to explain why visitors to Country Parks are drawn predominantly from higher social groups, higher income groups and from households where car-ownership is also high. Expressed in this way, as Curry (1985) remarks, Country Parks already provide what a particular market can stand but they do not address wider questions of social equity.

At a national level therefore it would seem that a site-based policy of recreation provision has had only a modest effect on redistributing where demand falls in the countryside and on providing genuinely new recreational opportunities that have wide appeal. Recreational facilities in most Country Parks do not cater for children's play, for outdoor sports or social gatherings other than those based on family groups. Moreover, local by-laws often restrict access for camping, caravanning, barbequeing, fishing, boating and the like. As a result most Country Parks offer little more than the kind of restrained enjoyment that has only transitory appeal to most people. The selective appeal of such provision is not necessarily class-based because members of all social and economic groups visit Country Parks and similar countryside sites, but by serving to restrict the range and diversity of recreational opportunities available, existing provision may discourage some people from visiting the countryside more frequently or from participating at all.

Attempts to promote activities and events in certain Country Parks have met with a measure of success when gauged by attendance figures at guided walks for example and special events. However, similar activities in other parks have not met with the same success (Countryside Commission, 1980b). In part this variable response arises because no two Country Parks are identical either in terms of their

105

facilities and staff or in terms of their environmental and social setting. It also reflects the fact that the catchments of some parks are more
localized than others. As a result, promoting events or activities will
not necessarily lead to increased use or socially beneficial use unless
some attempt is made to find out what appeals to the potential
constituencies a park can serve. The new policies for Country Parks
outlined by the Commission in 1987 recognize a requirement to
'define the interests and activities of the public they serve' but, at the
same time these policies provide no guidance about how these interests can be identified. To be effective, such policies will need to be
based on an understanding of people's recreational needs and of their
willingness and ability to participate and not just on an understanding
of the requirements of existing visitors. Without this understanding,
the culture of recreation permitted in Country Parks will continue to
be dominated by the attitudes and ideology of providers, managers
and that small percentage of the public who use them and not by the
needs of the wider public the parks purport to serve. At least in concept, Regional Parks were originally designed to provide a greater mix
of recreational experiences than those provided in Country Parks,
although they too have not lived up to expectations.

Regional Parks

The history of Regional Parks in Britain is a chequered one. In his
assessment of how leisure provision could meet the demands of the
Fourth Wave in 1964, Dower proposed Regional Parks as a means of
providing multiple leisure facilities in close proximity to the city, bas-
ing his recommendation on the experience and vision as he saw it of
Holland, Germany and North America (Civic Trust 1964).In Scotland,
Regional Parks formed an integral part of the national system of Parks
proposed in 1974 and they were recommended for England and Wales
by the Countryside Review Committee when it reported in 1977.

In practice few such parks exist and even in Scotland the so-called
'Clyde-Muirshiel Regional Park' had no statutory significance until
quite recently (Turner, 1985). The present expectation is that Regional
Parks in Scotland will be used as a means of protecting the rural setting of conurbations, much as Abercrombie had envisaged the role of
the 1940s 'outer scenic areas' (Countryside Commission Scotland,
1988). Their recreational role is hence likely to be secondary and subordinate to that of landscape interests and those of other primary land
uses such as agriculture and forestry. However, the desire on behalf of
some local authorities and landowners to improve the economy of
many rural areas through tourism and farm diversification will mean

that this position is likely to be challenged and in the absence of other concrete examples it is difficult to know what this type of designation is capable of achieving. In practice, each Regional Park has to be examined on its own merits for as Elson points out (Elson, 1986), the Lee Valley Regional Park (LVRP) with its designation as a separate statutory authority is very different from the Standing Conference mechanism used to administer the Colne Valley Regional Park to the west of London and the Joint Committees for other proposed Regional Parks such as the Sandwells area in the West Midlands. The LVRP has the longest and richest tradition in promoting a variety of recreational opportunities close to where demand lies and arguably it has also been the most successful one.

The Lee Valley Regional Park

As originally conceived by the Countryside Review Committee, Regional Parks were to provide a range of planned and organized leisure choices in an area, so that dispersal of demand would come about naturally and unobtrusively. They pointed to the Lee Valley Regional Park as a model for their proposals which they called 'County Leisure Parks'. This Regional Park had been created in 1966 by Act of Parliament to:

> 'procure or arrange for the development, improvement, preservation and management of the park as a place for the occupation of leisure, recreation, sport, games or amusement or similar activity, for the provision of nature reserves and for the provision and enjoyment of entertainments of any kind.'

Sponsored by three county councils – Hertfordshire, Essex and the former London County Council, the Park Authority raised income by a precept on the rates and by 1986 extended over some 23 miles (37km) from the edge of Ware in Hertfordshire southwards to near the Thames at Limehouse (Figure 5.6). By this date, the Park Authority had an interest (by way of freehold, leasehold or licence) over more than 3,000 acres (12,000 ha) which accounts for just over 30% of the total area. Approximately 28% of the area is water, including the navigable and recreational water ways of the Lee and Stort respectively and several reservoirs owned and managed by the regional water company (Thames Water Company). Extensive gravel workings and agricultural areas, together with land used for statutory services such as road, rail and power account for the remainder. The area hence embraces many of the traditional land-uses that typify the urban fringe and the whole of London's population lies within a radius of 25 miles (40km). With the abolition of the GLC in 1986, its 80% funding role was transferred to the 32 constituent London boroughs.

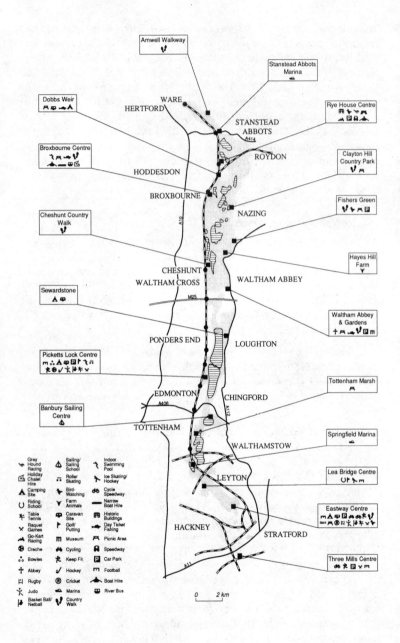

Figure 5.6: The Lee Valley Regional Park. Countryside and leisure facilities
Source: Lee Valley Regional Park Authority, 1986

The initial proposal anticipated that the authority would purchase all the land within its boundary in the belief that public ownership would provide the most effective means of achieving desirable results. This goal has not been achieved and the assumption that public ownership can achieve desirable land-use outcomes has also proved difficult to sustain. A recent review of the Lee Valley Park Plan undertaken in 1984 shows that like Country Parks, the LVPA had not been very successful in providing a clear identity for the Park either on the ground as would be visible through a distinctive 'park landscape' or through promotional activities which provided potential users with a distinctive 'recreational product'.

At the same time this review exposed weaknesses in the LVPA's ability to speed up the restoration and landscaping of mineral workings, to influence the activities of those statutory authorities which use the valley as a service corridor and its failure to improve access to and through the park by different constituencies of users eg: walkers, cyclists, recreational boaters, naturalists, white-water canoeists, surf-boarders, water-skiers. Consultation with members of the public and interested parties also revealed a reluctance on behalf of the authority to provide facilities for use by essentially local communities, especially those communities with no tradition of participation in sports or in visiting the countryside.

The new plan, serviced by a largely new management team seeks to address these shortcomings, but as Elson (1986) notes its approach based on a 'master-plan' stands in strong contrast to the more flexible approaches to area management evident elsewhere in the urban fringe (Chapter 7) especially in circumstances where the LVRPA has no direct power over development control. One sign that the LVRPA is sensitive to the need for a more flexible approach is provided through the involvement of the Countryside Commission as part of their urban-fringe initiatives. The appointment of a Community Projects Officer and the integration of the Rangers Section into the Countryside Service with its ambitious programme of countryside events are supported by the Commission. Most recently as part of the Commission's policy of improving information about countryside activities it has supported new marketing initiatives taken to improve public awareness of the Park and its leisure opportunities and, building on the experiences of Operation Gateway in Nottingham (see Chapter 6), it is also pursuing a number of initiatives designed to encourage community-wide use of the park.

Significant in the history of the park is the new emphasis that is given to wild-life conservation. In 1969 the original park plan anticipated that five Nature Reserves would be created although no systematic appraisal of sites for nature conservation had been undertaken. Recently several sites in the park have been surveyed and the NCC now has notified four Sites of Special Scientific Interest. Several Areas of Nature Conservation Importance have been identified in the new plan and the authority plans to manage seven areas as nature reserves, though not necessarily by themselves. The recognition given to wildlife conservation as both a legitimate land-use in its own right and as material consideration to be taken into account by the authority when appraising developments in the park, is consistent with maintaining the authority's broad concern for the environment of the park. But, implementing such proposals will require a flexible approach especially on sites where nature conservation interests and recreational interests conflict – as on several of the reservoirs (Sidaway, 1988). On these sites where the Thames Water Company is encouraged to provide facilities that are self-financing, nature conservation interests may only be secured if the park authority or others are prepared to pay for them.

As well as demonstrating a broad concern for the upgrading of the landscape of the park, the LVRPA has also made strenuous efforts to provide a wide range of outdoor activities and indoor sports facilities in the park. Over 40 different sports are catered for with many of these facilities being designed for all-weather use and for use by disadvantaged groups, for example, the disabled, ethnic minorities and mothers with young children. Over 2 million people used the activity centres shown in Figure 5.6 and their home addresses fall predominantly in the Greater London area. Two of the facilities to show an increase in use are the Dobbs Weir and Sewardstone Caravan Parks where national and international tourists are strongly represented in the annual use figures. The proposal that the Authority should establish heritage and visitor centres throughout the park is also regarded as a means of increasing this tourist trade – an aspect of recreational use that is beginning to assume importance in Regional Parks in Scotland as well.

The Lee Valley Regional Park has come a long way since the early proposals made by the Civic Trust for what amounted to little more than several Country Parks located in the same area. The advantage that the ad hoc LVRPA has over other approaches to recreation provision is that its source of funding is predictable, it has an identifiable statutory role and its tradition of leisure provision has embraced a wide range of informal and formal activities. Its accountability to a wide constituency however is likely to prove of growing concern. Some London boroughs already feel that disproportionate attention has been given to outer London at the expense of more needy inner

London boroughs and their disadvantaged communities. Certainly the physical environment of the south with its extensive areas of derelict land and poorly developed access to river courses and reservoirs contrasts markedly with the pleasant, rural environment of Ware in the north with its numerous footpaths, bridleways and nature reserves. The Plan itself pays little attention to the different local constituencies these areas are likely to serve or to their different needs, but at least the Authority provides a statutory forum through which these differences can be discussed and provides a formal and enduring mechanism for securing co-ordinated provision. Without the presence and persistence of the LVRP authority it is unlikely that for example the British Waterways Board would have agreed to a thirty-year period over which the authority can carry out work on the Lee Navigation Towpath to improve the amenity value of some 23 miles (36km) of riverside walk. The fact that work started first in Hackney provides some measure of the sensitivity of the authority to the needs of particular communities.

Central government's insistence that local authority leisure services are placed on a competitive basis, means that the regional recreational role of the LVRP will come under closer scrutiny than in the past. Because funding now comes from 32 different London boroughs and because at times of financial hardship all public authorities will come to review the effectiveness of their contribution, questions about the extent to which rate-payers in each London borough benefit will be raised. Under these circumstances, reaching agreement about the effectiveness of new policies is likely to prove more difficult than in the recent past when the GLC was the major financial provider.

In so far as the LVRPA has been able to provide a planned and organized set of leisure choices close to where demand lies, then it has perhaps emphasized formal sports provision rather than provision of a more informal kind. Moreover within the provision for informal recreation it has emphasized quiet and contemplative uses of the countryside favoured by some people rather than a more active involvement with the city's countryside through events and social occasions which are favoured by other constituencies of users. 'Opening up the Park' for informal recreation has now become one of the guiding policies for the authority and reinforces a more promotional approach to countryside recreation that could be adopted elsewhere in the urban fringe (see Chapter 7). It will be instructive to examine which constituencies of users benefit from the new programme of activities and provision favoured by the new management team and to record how successful this approach is at reconciling the potentially disparate views of its pay-masters. Under these circumstances the 'Master Plan' agreed upon by the LVRPA may not provide a realistic means of reconciling the competing claims of local and regional constituencies or of reconciling their differing views about what constitutes appropriate recreational use of the 'country-side in the city'. The experience of other Regional Parks such as the Colne Valley, reveals similar tensions and competing claims.

The Colne Valley Regional Park

The Colne Valley Regional Park (CVRP) covers an area of some 40 square miles along the valley of the river Colne from Rickmansworth in the north to the River Thames at Staines in the south – a distance of 14 miles (22km). The local authorities began studying the recreational potential of the area in detail in 1965 at the height of the period when recreation demand was expected to quadruple in a generation. The area offered scope for water-based recreation on the wet gravel workings and lying within 16 miles (25km) of central London was also regarded as offering Londoners a range of countryside facilities such as walking, picnicking, riding, camping and birdwatching. The park falls within 11 local authorities but unlike the Lee Valley Regional Park which has its own specially created authority, the CVRP was conceived as a more informal, and less costly, collaborative venture. It is overseen by the Standing Conference on the Colne Valley (SCCVRP) and received support from the Countryside Commission. The Standing Conference is comprised of two elected members from each of the authorities and is serviced by an officer working party.

The SCCVRP agreed upon a strategic plan for the park in 1971. Introducing the plan, the chairman of the Standing Conference recommended it to the local authorities for their formal adoption because 'it will preserve the rural atmosphere of the park while providing the right kind of facilities.' (Foreword, Colne Valley – Strategy for a Regional Park, 1972). This plan provided a framework of policies within which authorities could prepare more detailed short term plans for action. Throughout the early part of the 1970s little progress was made in implementing these policies and in 1978 the Standing Conference sought support from the Countryside Commission for a countryside management project to assist with its implementation. The objectives of this project were to:

- enhance the landscape of the Colne Valley by encouraging better management of the existing landscape and promoting landscape improvements;
- develop the potential for informal recreation;
- safeguard productive agriculture and woodland;

※ ensure proper consideration of wildlife conservation;

※ promote a management and implementation framework co-ordinated with the strategic framework already provided in the plan.

In essence the broad concept of the park is the provision of rural as opposed to urban recreation within a countryside setting and the countryside management project is a means of carrying out some of the practical work required to achieve these ends. However, a persistent and enduring concern of the Standing Conference in its discussions and recommendations has been its desire to restrict the development of noisy water sports on the worked out gravel pits. Many of these water-sports have gained in popularity over the life of the park but are not the kind of recreational pursuits which are regarded as acceptable to local residents. As a result recreation, other than that of the quiet contemplative kind, appears to be regarded as 'inappropriate development'. So although the countryside management project was an attempt to provide a new impetus and identity to the park, it did so essentially by emphasising the promotion of information and by undertaking basic survey work of habitats such as woodlands and hedgerows rather than examining what new recreational initiatives might be pursued.

When a new strategy and broadsheet was revised in 1985 it identified a number of major schemes for implementation over an eight year period, including a park centre, other recreation centres (use unspecified), and a network of bridle and cycleways. The recent establishment of the Colne Valley Park Groundwork Trust in 1987 (see Chapter 7) is intended to provide an effective and viable countryside management service in the park. By drawing upon local authority support and commercial funds it hopes to raise additional resources for the park and by working with the voluntary bodies it seeks to stimulate a greater commitment to the enterprise by local residents than has been apparent to date. Although there has been some improvements in recreation provision in the park in recent years, in contrast to the Lee Valley Regional Park, attempts to provide a combination of formal and informal recreation facilities throughout the park have been modest. As a result, the emphasis on the ruralization of the landscape, nature conservation and quiet recreation activities means that a rural atmosphere of the area may well have been preserved at the expense of an effective recreational role.

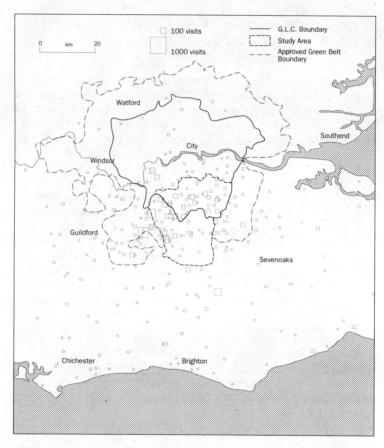

Figure 5.7: Destinations of other trips made to countryside sites by visitors interviewed at survey sites in the South London Green Belt area
Source: Roberts and Thompson, 1981

A socially beneficial role for recreation sites in the urban fringe?

Any social benefits to be derived from Country and Regional Parks were expected to result from locating provision close to demand, and in aggregate, provision focused in urban fringes does accord with the overall pattern of demand. For example, a study of the destinations of the most recent visit undertaken by respondents in the 1981 *National Survey of Countryside Recreation* showed that 40% of these destinations lay in the urban area or within 1 km of it (Sidaway and Duffield,

1981). An additional 22% fell in the countryside around towns. By contrast, only 16% of destinations fell in the more distant countryside (10 km from an urban area). Likewise at a sub-regional scale, a study of visitors to informal recreation sites in a southern sector of the London green belt (Roberts and Thompson, 1981, Harrison, 1983) revealed that the destinations of other countryside sites visited by respondents fell predominantly in or close to the urban area. Destinations in the more distant countryside and on the coasts were less numerous (Figure 5.7). In these terms the urban fringe and urban parks are more heavily used than the deeper countryside. However, several studies reveal that the presumed accessibility of recreation sites in the urban fringe to people who do not have access to a car and to people who live in inner city areas, is ill-founded.

In a survey of visitors to several recreation sites in the south London Green Belt, Harrison, (1981 and 1983) found that whilst on average 75% of visitors arrived by car, the percentage arriving by other means varied from 3% to 54%. On its own, distance from the urban area did not readily account for this variability save only that the more distant sites (>5kms from the urban area) had the highest number of visitors who arrived by car. The study also showed that on average 47% of those people who had not arrived by car, did not have access to one and this percentage rose to 61% at one site. Moreover, most of these visitors arrived on foot rather than by public transport. Neither the assumed accessibility of recreation sites in the urban fringe to those people who are dependent on public transport nor their accessibility to inner city residents was substantiated by this study. In practice, inner city residents never formed more than 10% of the total visitors at any site (Figure 5.8).

However, these findings do suggest that sites in urban fringe locations are accessible to some people who do not have access to a car as long as sites are located within walking distance and local residents are familiar with public transport routes and services. Groome and Tarrant (1984) for example suggest that public transport services to Country Parks are effective over comparatively short distances (5–8 km) even on long established routes. Any socially-beneficial role urban-fringe sites were expected to play through their accessibility to people who do not own cars appears to have been achieved in the context of an essentially local population. The Study of Four Parks undertaken in Scotland across an urban to rural continuum reinforces this finding (Tourism and Recreation Research Unit, 1980).

This detailed study shows that a park's location in relation to the distribution, density and social composition of a local population has a profound effect on the kind of use a site receives. Critically this study

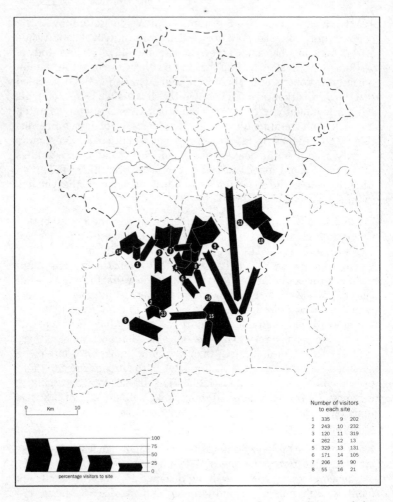

Figure 5.8: Number and origins of visitors to sites in South London green belt
Source: Harrison, 1981

found that much of the use a park receives is determined by those who walk to it. Figure 5.9 shows that although the catchment areas of parks overlap, 60% of visitors are drawn from localized catchments of about 2 km. Within this 60% catchment the locations of those areas contributing most visitors to each park reflects the geography of settlement in the surrounding area. By contrast, the social and economic characteristics of park users who do not live near a park are similar to

116

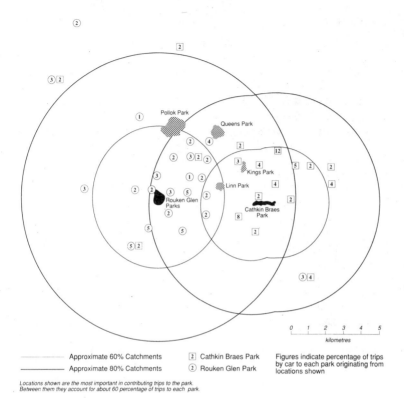

Approximate 60% Catchments   2 Cathkin Braes Park   Figures indicate percentage of trips
by car to each park originating from
Approximate 80% Catchments   ② Rouken Glen Park   locations shown

Locations shown are the most important in contributing trips to the park.
Between them they account for about 60 percentage of trips to each park.

Figure 5.9: Catchments of two parks
Source: TRRU, 1980

each other. They show a predominance of young adults in non-manu-
al occupations and relatively few school children, when compared to
local users. As has been shown by numerous other studies these differences are likely to be a reflection of the high level of car-ownership
enjoyed by this group and the resultant ease with which many sites in
the urban and urban fringe area can be reached. The study concludes
that where a park is located with respect to a local population often
living within 2–5km will determine in the first instance the type of use
that parks receives. In the light of these findings it is clear that the precise location of a Country Park means that some parks can play a more
effective social role than others.

Conclusion

The substantial financial burden Country Parks represent for the public sector, means that their recreational role is likely to come under additional scrutiny now that leisure services provided by local authorities are subject to competitive tendering (Benington and White, 1988). It is therefore important to know how these sites contribute to people's enjoyment of the countryside and to establish whether the original assumptions made about their recreational role apply in the changing context of the 1990s. Those studies reviewed in this chapter suggest that many of the original assumptions upon which the recreational role of Country Parks were based are untenable. Assumptions about the accessibility of urban-fringe parks to 'disadvantaged' sections of the public are largely unfounded and the popular appeal of managed sites rather than the wider countryside, is also not substantiated. However, these studies do show that provision in urban fringe locations accords well with the pattern of expressed demand and they provide some support for the revised policies for Country Parks (Countryside Commission, 1987c) which assert that decisions on future management and provision of Country Parks 'must rest on carefully defining the interests and activities of the public they serve'. In particular these studies show that before such a policy can be implemented effectively, providers and park staff will need to discover what recreational role a park can serve for those constituencies defined primarily by a park's precise location. In some cases this is likely to mean that the dominant culture of provision traditionally associated with Country Parks will need to be reassessed if the park is to serve its local public well. It might also require involving the commercial sector in both the provision of facilities and appropriate transport links. The need for an appraisal of these latter aspects of provision is explored in Chapter 6.

6

Public transport and countryside recreation

....

Introduction

Policies designed to improve and promote public transport services for leisure journeys recommend themselves on several accounts. First, these policies may persuade some people who visit the country-side regularly to leave their cars at home and so reduce congestion and pollution. Second, by promoting some sites rather than others members of this same group may be encouraged to visit new destinations. As a result some re-distribution of use may occur. Third, by improving public transport to the countryside around towns some people who had previously not visited the countryside might be encouraged to participate. In this way improving the accessibility of the urban-fringe might bring social benefits which a site-based policy on its own would not necessarily achieve. This chapter examines the efficacy of public transport policies designed to influence recreational behaviour and to raise participation levels amongst people who have no recent recent tradition of visiting the countryside.

Public transport and countryside recreation

During the immediate post-war period a heavy decline in passenger traffic took place throughout the public transport system and by 1973 just under 80% of all passenger mileage in Britain was undertaken by private transport (Figure 6.1). However, the changing political and economic climate of the mid-70s led to a reassessment of the role of public transport. At this time traffic congestion in towns and the pol-lution associated with it prompted many urban planners to look close-ly at traffic management schemes and the role of public transport in them. Furthermore, by the mid-seventies energy prices and inflation

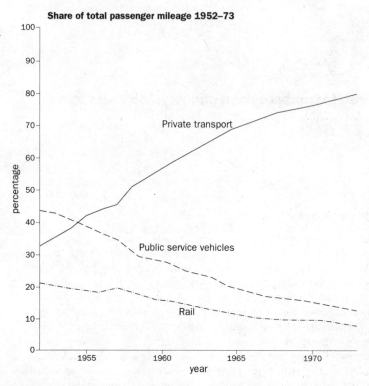

Figure 6.1: Share of total passenger mileage, 1952–73
Source: Countryside Commission, 1976

were increasing and several urban authorities looked to the public transport system as a means of promoting energy conservation as well. At this time, a Labour government was favourably disposed to socially-responsible transport policies based on public subsidy which included the cross-subsidizing of rural services by revenue earned from the urban network. All of these trends led to a more positive approach to public transport and by 1976 a report to the Countryside Commission (1976a) on public transport for countryside recreation identified a degree of stability in public transport services which specific recreational travel services could build upon.

In practice, recreational travel had not formed a significant part of public transport once private motor vehicles became available to a mass market and numerous surveys at sites in the countryside confirmed that up to 90% of visitors had travelled by private transport. Studies such as those reviewed by Elson (1979) show that the number of visitors arriving at sites by public transport seldom rose above 3–4%. Transport operators regard leisure travel as a problem because it is highly seasonal and concentrated on week-ends. Their main revenue is derived from the predictable demand generated by commuters, school journeys and commerce (Cracknell, 1967). However, a number of special schemes for recreational use of public transport were undertaken in the early 1970s and 1980s using trains, buses and special mini-buses often subsidized by public authorities (Greening and Slater, 1984). Special recreational services included a bus link along the South Wales coast, a Roman Wall Tourist Bus in the border country, the Peak Pathfinder based on mini-buses in the Peak District and a similar service called the Snowdon Sherpa in North Wales. In reviewing these and other schemes the Dart study identified several objectives which could be pursued by organizations wishing to develop recreational travel:

* provision of access to the countryside for those people who do not own, have the use of, or wish to use a private car;

* provision of recreational transport to parts of the countryside which are either not accessible to the private car or are specially vulnerable to wear and intrusive road construction;

* opening up new opportunities for recreational travel by improving links in an otherwise fragmented recreational network;

* offering a new recreational experience in its own right;

* assisting in the maintenance of a rural public transport network for the benefit of the rural population; and

* making more efficient use of resources such as land and energy and reducing environmental pollution.

Of these several objectives some are designed to protect the resource, some to widen participation by groups of people who might otherwise not participate in visits to the countryside, some to enhance recreational experiences and yet others to contribute to a broader strategy for integrated rural and urban development. Importantly the last two objectives need to be linked to other development strategies if they are to succeed because the desire to improve rural transport services starts with the needs of a rural population rather than an urban population and recreational travel is not likely to be the primary determinant of such schemes. More recently, to these objectives has been added another – fulfilling the needs and requirements of the tourist industry both as an employer and the needs of overseas tourists who may not be prepared to use a private car to visit countryside destinations (Countryside Commission,1987d).

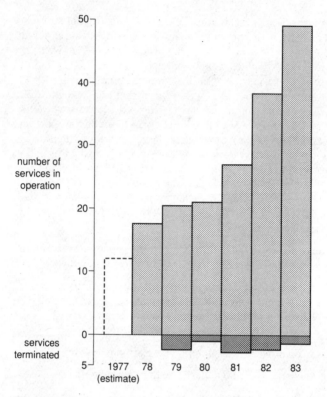

Figure 6.2: Increase in number of recreational transport services 1978–83
Source: Groome and Tarrant, 1984

Experience with subsidized public transport schemes

Since the DART report appeared in 1976 several public authorities have subsidized transport services in rural areas and Groome and Tarrant's study (1984) suggests that between 1978 and 1983 about half the county councils in England and Wales have supported directly or promoted such schemes. Almost two thirds of the transport schemes included in this study had been specifically created and planned for recreational use although half the schemes failed to generate the levels of traffic anticipated at the outset. The most successful services appeared to depend on a well established flow of tourist traffic and upon patronage and support of voluntary groups such as the Ramblers' Association. All the schemes depended upon subsidies of one kind or another and recreational traffic served only to cover the operating costs of existing transport services. Groome and Tarrant's study also shows that approximately one sixth of those recreational travel services which had started up since 1978 had been abandoned. (Figure 6.2).

More critical to the attainment of the recreational objectives associated with such schemes was their limited success in raising participation among inner city residents and amongst people without access to a car. Most progress has been made in promoting schemes either in the more remote countryside beyond the urban area or in tourist areas such as the National Parks. So for example the Sevenoaks Rambler and the Kent Rambler followed circular routes in the Kent countryside and the Gwent Sunday Bus Experiment did well because there was an established tradition of tourism in the area (Greening and Slater, 1984). Rather less progress had been made in widening the choice of recreational opportunities in the countryside adjacent to urban areas or in providing new links between urban networks and rural services. However, by the 1980s several urban authorities were committed to maintaining a public transport system and to promoting new travel arrangements which could benefit leisure trips. One such project undertaken in Greater Manchester and West Yorkshire – the Wayfarer project (Countryside Commission, 1985), throws light on the potential of public transport as a 'social service'.

The Wayfarer project

The Wayfarer project was a recreational transport experiment sponsored by the Countryside Commission and supported by the Public Transport Executives of West Yorkshire County Council (WYCC) and the former Greater Manchester Council (GMC). It was designed to establish the opportunities for 'greater use, for recreational purposes, of existing public transport services' and involved a sophisticated approach to marketing recreational travel over a period of three and a half years starting in 1981 (Table 6.1). From the outset, the project benefited enormously from an established integrated public transport network which linked bus and rail services across urban and rural boundaries and from popular through tickets like the 'Day Rovers' which were self-cancelling and could be purchased in advance. Additionally, the potential demand for public transport was high because both unemployment and non-car ownership amongst urban residents were well above the national average. Furthermore, both the WYCC and the GMC had taken initiatives during the 1970s and 1980s to secure a number of recreational sites close to the urban area. Several Country Parks lie on the perimeter of Manchester and these together with the proximity of the Peak District National Park and the West Pennine Moors provided extensive areas of fine countryside in close

123

Table 6.1: Summary of main Wayfarer initiatives in Greater Manchester
Source: Countryside Commission, 1985

Objective	Year	Initiative	Summary
Promoting the existing network	1981	Adventure Rider Club	Club aimed at encouraging travel by the under 15s, with newsletter, organised trips and competitions
		Wayfarer Walk (Peak Border)	First of series of leaflets on linear country-side walks in Greater Manchester using local bus services
	1982	Wayfarer Walk (Saddleworth)	Publication of two further leaflets in series (see above)
		Wayfarer Walk (Bobs Lane Ferry)	
		Explorer programme from Manchester	Input of publicity material for standard Explorer programme prepared by National Bus Company
		Discover Cheshire from Manchester	Input of publicity material for leaflet prepared by Cheshire County Council encouraging use of public transport
		BBC Radio Manchester	Weekly broadcast on local radio, offering suggestions for day trips to the countryside from Manchester using local buses and trains
	1982-4	Countryside information on Bus Guides	Inclusion of information on country parks and other countryside sites on selected Bus Guides (i.e. timetables) where space permits
	1983	Countryside Collection	Booklet of suggested itineraries for day visits to the countryside, based on talks given on BBC Radio Manchester (see above)
		Wayfarer Walk (Peak Forest Canal)	Publication of two further leaflets in series (see above)
		Wayfarer Walk (Ashworth Valley & Cheesden Brook)	
		Wayfarer Travel Club	Launch of club aimed at users of the Peak Wayfarer ticket (see below) with membership and newsletter for all who completed a travel questionnaire in the Peak Wayfarer Handbook giving details of their journeys
		Travel Club Days Out	Escorted tours and guided walks to selected destinations for members of Greater Manchester Travel Clubs
	1983-4	Student and local newspapers	Newspaper features to promote the use of public transport for recreation, including promotion of the Peak Wayfarer ticket (see below)
	1984	Wayfarer Walk (Lower Tame Valley)	Publication of two further leaflets in series (see above)
		Wayfarer Walk (Norden, Catley Lane Head & Healey))	
		Tame Valley	First two in a series of comprehensive leaflets covering the river valley system in Greater Manchester, with countryside and public transport information
		Croal-Irwell Valley	
		Five Days Out by Peak Wayfarer	Set of ten leaflets, each giving itineraries for five suggested day trips from major towns in Greater Manchester, using Peak Wayfarer tickets, with details of bus routes and times
		Bramall Hall	Promotional leaflet for historic house, with bus service information and discount on admission charge for bus passengers
		Bolton's Countryside by Bus	Leaflets promoting access by bus to the local countryside around Greater Manchester
		Dunham Massey and the Cheshire Borderland by Bus	

Objective	Year	Initiative	Summary
Through tickets	1982	Peak Wayfarer ticket	Launch of day runabout ticket covering Greater Manchester, East Cheshire and the Peak District, with associated leaflets, posters, map folder and handbook with suggested itineraries
	1983-4	Peak Wayfarer ticket	Re-launch of day runabout ticket (see above) extended to include additional bus services, including National Express services
Special recreational services	1982	Wythenshawe-Tatton Park 293	New bus service linking an area of low car ownership in South Manchester with stately home and country park
		Manchester-Castleton 395 Glossop-Hayfield 396	New bus services linking Manchester with the Peak District National Park
	1983	Wythenshawe-Tatton Park 293 Manchester-Castleton 395 Glossop-Hayfield 396	Repeat of services operated in 1982
		Macclesfield-Jodrell Bank E70	New bus service providing access to stately home (Capesthorne Hall) and the radio telescope at Jodrell Bank
		Horwich-Lever Park 516	Extension of existing service to provide access to popular recreational area in West Pennine Moors
	1984	Wythenshawe-Tatton Park 293 Manchester-Castleton 395	Repeat of services operated in 1982-83
		Glossop-Hayfield 360	Repeat of service operated (as 396) in 1982-83
		Macclesfield-Jodrell Bank E70	Repeat of service operated in 1983
		Horwich-Lever Park 516	Repeat of service operated in 1983
Other initiatives	1981-84	BBC Radio Manchester BBC Radio 4	Occasional broadcasts on national and local radio drawing attention to opportunities for recreational travel by public transport
		Talks and lectures	Promotion of Wayfarer project and recreational transport by talks and lectures to university, voluntary and other groups and to adult education classes
	1984	College of Adult Education Open Days	Open days for the general public, with talks and exhibitions, stressing opportunities for leisure travel by public transport in the Greater Manchester area

proximity to the 2.6 million inhabitants of Greater Manchester and at least in theory, accessible to them. Taken together, these environmental resources and a commitment by the two transport executives to promote recreational travel suggested a favourable context within which the scheme might flourish and through which people who were recreationally 'disadvantaged' might benefit.

A wide-ranging initiative such as the Wayfarer project impinges on several aspects of leisure travel and behaviour and as a result it is difficult to evaluate people's response to one aspect of leisure travel such as visits to the countryside. Neither is it easy to identify how specific groups of people have responded. However, the published report (Countryside Commission, 1985b) suggests several indicators by which its performance as a social service can be judged.

Central to the whole approach to the Wayfarer project was its use of target-marketing techniques through which particular age groups, income groups or interest groups could be reached. Amongst those groups who traditionally do not participate in countryside recreation to the extent that might be expected from their presence in the population as a whole, are young adults, the elderly, ethnic minorities, single-parent families, people on low incomes and the unemployed. Some of the initiatives undertaken during the project were specifically aimed at these groups. For example, the under-sixteens already benefited from a flat-rate fare for single journeys and they represented a ready-made market for recreational travel. An Adventure Rider Club based on free membership of a club and a travel pack distributed through bus stations, rail stations and schools encouraged children to take a greater interest in the countryside and the environment and promoted group travel on lesser used routes. In the first six months 30,000 children joined the scheme and this membership level was maintained for three years. The continuing interest of teachers, youth leaders and youth clubs provided some indication of the extent to which there might be longer term benefits to local communities as well. Similarly an education project started by WYCC led to five district education authorities collaborating with a specialist firm of educational publishers and promoters to provide transport and environmental projects that were tied in with school work. At the same time young people benefited by gaining confidence in using the transport network.

Building on the success of the Adventure Rider Club, a Travel Clubs section was established within Greater Manchester Transport aimed at providing a package of services to a wide market. Attractive destinations and their associated events and facilities which could be reached by public transport were promoted. One of the most successful of these clubs was the Travel Companions Club aimed at the over fifties. Car-ownership amongst the elderly is generally lower than for other age groups and physical disabilities among the elderly mean that the support of helpers is required before journeys are likely to be entered into. Through the Travel Companions Club some 60,000 people came to enjoy outings to the countryside and its membership continued to grow.

Schemes designed to reach other recreationally disadvantaged groups have also been pursued through collaboration with the voluntary sector. In a small-scale project supported by Keighly Council, for example, through collaboration between the Voluntary Service and its Community Transport Organiser, a small group of people came to meet once a fortnight to go on easy local walks and on visits to places of interest by public transport. Participants were encouraged to join by voluntary organisers familiar with the existing voluntary groups. A similar objective was pursued in Greater Manchester when the opportunity arose for linking an attractive country house, Tatton Park, with one of the poorest housing estates in the area at Wythenshawe. Tatton Park is managed by two authorities, the National Trust and Cheshire County Council and was poorly served by public transport. Together these authorities guaranteed payment for a new contract bus service which ran on Sundays and Bank Holidays to the park and hall. A survey of 108 people interviewed during five days in August 1984 suggested that 93% of the passengers did not have access to a private motor vehicle and 67% indicated that they would not have visited Tatton Park had the bus service not been operating; many people would have stayed at home and only 12% indicated that they would have made the effort to get there by other means. Improving both the accessibility of the destination and its promotion as a location in which numerous activities and events took place had encouraged 59% of the respondents to visit for the first time and the overwhelming majority said that they intended to repeat the trip.

Most of the projects aimed at specific groups of people were designed to use existing transport services and marketing these services provided the key to their success. Just how crucial a sustained marketing effort is to the success of such schemes is evidenced by the demise of the Wakefield Countryside bus which declined dramatically when the service ceased to be marketed. Both transport executives involved in the Wayfarer project were convinced that the success of these schemes is only as good as their marketing. In general terms approximately 1.2% of the executives' budget was invested in marketing the scheme. Such a proportion compares favourably with most large commercial organizations who can devote up to 15% of their budgets to marketing. Both participating councils assert that more people have become aware of the public transport network during the life of the project. Total passenger traffic increased, and several schemes continued to be supported after the project itself had ended.

It is less easy to determine how much of this traffic took the form of the recreational travel the Wayfarer project sought to promote, although the report asserts that many more recreational trips were being made on both sides of the Pennines during the life of the project. Other transport initiatives taken at the same time such as cheap off-peak fares will have contributed to increased use of the network and changes in the amount of leisure time available may also have raised participation levels. The experimental nature of many of the individual projects together with their small scale and short life span also means that it is difficult to assess whether or not there has been any permanent change in leisure travel amongst the population as a whole, especially amongst those groups of people who are unaccustomed to recreational travel. At the same time, the project has served to demonstrate that the professional promotion of recreational travel through the public transport network had encouraged some people to leave their cars at home when making a trip to the countryside. It has also provided pleasure to many thousands of people by creating a recreational experience in its own right. Travelling by bus, train and boat can be enjoyed as part of a range of experiences and when linked to competitions, projects and school work and to special events undertaken in the company of friends, the whole may well prove to have an enduring effect on people's leisure behaviour and attitudes.

Both authorities are convinced that as a result of the Wayfarer Project, the general public has a heightened awareness of recreational travel opportunities available through the public transport network. Whether or not this heightened awareness will be translated into raised participation in countryside trips and to positive attitudes towards the countryside remains to be seen. What is undeniable is that considerable latent demand for recreational travel based on a public transport network exists and a sustained and co-ordinated approach to marketing the recreational opportunities accessible by public transport is one means of tapping it.

Other public transport initiatives

The Wayfarer Project was initiated for a variety of reasons not least those concerned with generating more passenger traffic on routes that were operating below capacity. In other words most recreational services promoted existing facilities and routes and operated at marginal cost. As a consequence, the recreational opportunities promoted through the project were those 'constrained' by the existing network and by any improvements in accessibility a vigorous marketing of the network could achieve. None of these marketing initiatives are new to professionals in the field of transport services but the project also looked at novel ways of marketing recreational travel to make it attractive to particular target groups who lived in the urban area. The Travel Clubs were a direct outcome of this target marketing approach. However, although it is possible to segment passenger markets into different groups, by age or income for example, finding out what appeals to each age group requires an intimate knowledge of people's motives and their attitudes to both recreation and the countryside.

Because there is a dearth of information about people's leisure preferences, especially those concerned with informal recreation such as
countryside recreation, successful marketing strategies need to be
informed by research into people's attitudes, values and motives for
undertaking trips to the countryside. This is true especially if people
have no recent tradition of visiting the countryside. One such study
which incorporated in-depth research is that undertaken by the
Leisure Services Division of Nottingham County Council and called
'Operation Gateway'.

Operation Gateway

Operation Gateway was launched in June 1983 and aimed:

> 'to investigate the demand from special groups for countryside recreation,
> and to assist in the provision of appropriate services and facilities that will
> enable and encourage members of these groups to visit the countryside.'
> (Le Motte, 1984).

Amongst that 25% of the population who do not visit the countryside,
the Nottingham study focused on those people who did not own a car,
were on low incomes and were single-parent families. The pilot stage
of the project involved the conduct of four discussion groups. Two
groups of up to eight respondents each were recruited from neighbourhoods in the inner city and two others were recruited from areas
on the outskirts of Nottingham. All the respondents had expressed
some interest in visiting the countryside when they were recruited.
The first stage of the study was carried out by professional market
researchers specialising in qualitative research and was designed to
explore various aspects of leisure behaviour and awareness of recreational opportunities in the countryside. The topics discussed in each
group covered the following themes: current leisure activities, incidence of trip-making to the countryside, awareness and use of
Country Parks, town parks and the wider countryside, barriers to
countryside trips and the potential for countryside trips. The second
stage of the project – the implementation stage – involved a labour
intensive, community-based approach through which specific leisure
travel initiatives were promoted. It was implemented by two project
workers funded by the Countryside Division of Leisure Services and
the Countryside Commission.

One of the main findings of the group discussions was that although
the cost of leisure travel was the first reason people mentioned as a
barrier to participation, equally important was the fact that people did
not know where to go in the countryside or how to get there. Few
respondents knew about Country Parks including popular areas such

as Sherwood Forest, few knew about the network of public transport services which could take them out into the countryside and many expressed considerable anxieties about using them – especially to places people were unfamiliar with. Respondents were much happier about the idea of going on organised coach outings because the outing could be anticipated and planned for in advance and a special coach trip seemed to offer a sense of security and confidence. In most groups the respondents wanted someone else to organize the trips because they felt they did not have the expertise to do it themselves. Community Centres and local schools were suggested as a good places for publicising trips for families and for groups of older children in particular. It was agreed that such trips could relieve the boredom of the school holidays which both children and adults experienced.

In summarizing the findings of this preliminary research phase, the consultants reported that although respondents wanted to make trips to the countryside, 'to get them into the habit of making trips will require a great deal of effort publicising where they can go and organising the trips so that they can get there.' (Phase 1 Report p.5). Through the group discussions it had become clear that although cheap transport might remove one constraint on participation, other community services would need to be employed as well if recreational trips were to become enjoyable experiences for people who had no tradition of countryside visiting.

The implementation stage of the project sought to build on these findings by using a community-based approach to promoting outings to the countryside. Two project workers undertook the task of providing local organisers with information and advice about possible destinations and usually arranged the transport. The onus for promoting the trips and selling tickets however, was put on local organisers. In this way a 'self-help' approach to community services was encouraged. It was also hoped that the experience provided by the Operation Gateway project might have an enduring effect by giving people sufficient confidence to organise their own trips at a later date. The project officers were directed to encourage participation by 'non-joiners', so that any overlap with other voluntary groups and agencies was minimized and as a means of extending the community-wide basis of participation.

Seventeen trips were completed over the short life of the project (six months) and a total of 328 people went on them. All trips were subsidized at the level of £1.09 per head. This figure includes the costs of publicity, admissions and meals where appropriate but excludes the salaries of temporary and permanent staff. Trips were organised by coach and mini-bus to Sherwood Forest and Ruffold Country Park and to the wider countryside around Dovedale and the Peak District, and on foot to Leen Valley Country Park. Organising trips by public transport rather than private hire proved much more difficult. For example when a trip was arranged on public transport – the Sherwood Forester, for a group who had already enjoyed a coach excursion to the countryside, only fifteen out of an anticipated party of seventy arrived at the bus station. Even when the bus was diverted to people's homes, the organisers were unable to encourage people to join them.

Most of the organised trips involved the wider community although a few were run for groups with specific needs, such as the disabled. Catering for the special requirements of these latter groups proved to be much more demanding than for the community-based trips. The community trips could be structured and adapted during the visit but three trips organised for senior citizens to Rufford Country Park exposed the inadequacy of the centre's facilities for catering for a large group of elderly people, even at times when few other visitors were present. Similar difficulties could be anticipated at destinations not used to experiencing sudden influxes of large numbers of people or to the requirements of particular visitor age groups, such as young adults, small children and disabled people. The most enjoyable trips to Country Park destinations were those organised around identifiable events and on occasions when the host ranger arranged specific activities for the groups. Less enjoyable were the trips on ordinary days when no events took place.

On this evidence it seemed that the low-key provision of facilities in the Country Park typified by a pleasant natural environment and peace and quiet was not sufficient to sustain people's enjoyment of a trip. As the then Marketing Officer of the Countryside Services remarked, this limited appeal has important implications for staffing, facilities provided in Country Parks and also for the attitudes of providers and their rangers – in other words the 'culture of Country Park provision' has limited appeal. It also suggests that people enjoy doing a range of activities when out in the countryside some of which could perhaps be provided in open spaces in the urban area itself. Moreover Country Parks tend to be adult-orientated destinations and some parents were unable to enjoy themselves because of the demands made on them by dissatisfied children. In practice therefore, what is provided at the destination contributed enormously to the total enjoyment of the trip and being out in a Country Park did not seem to provide the range of pleasurable experiences most people wanted. Under these circumstances it is unlikely that most people would wish to repeat their visit. Significantly, when one community undertook to organise its own outing, the trip went to Blackpool

Illuminations – a destination different in kind and character from those which Operation Gateway was designed to promote. It is a telling comment too on what the public and providers mean by a 'trip to the countryside'.

As with many of the initiatives taken with the Wayfarer Project, those taken by Operation Gateway were largely short term and experimental in character and it is hence difficult to draw general conclusions from them. The second report of the Gateway project emphasizes the uniqueness of many of the events in terms of their organisation, the destinations visited, the composition of the party and the weather conditions on the day of the outing. The project however demonstrated that in reality the cost of going on a trip to the countryside is often an excuse for not participating rather than a constraint. People did pay £2.00 per adult and £1.50 for a child on some trips plus money for refreshments and souvenirs but there would be a limit to how often this level of spending could be afforded by poor families. In practice, the project showed that the fear of price resistance can be overcome if sufficient enthusiasm is generated by local organizers and the prospect of an enjoyable day out includes a range of events which appeals to all age ranges. Information on its own was not sufficient to overcome the cost 'constraint' – a fact that was exemplified by the poor response to a letter inviting local people to contact project workers (by Freepost) to find out about 'cheap trips to the countryside'. Only four out of 23 replied, and only one response led to a trip being organised and that at the second attempt.

The experience gained through Operation Gateway about people's attitudes to the countryside and trips to it serves to emphasize that connecting people to the pleasures of countryside recreation involves more than promoting destinations accessible by the public transport network. Providers and organizations seeking to raise the level of countryside visiting and environmental awareness amongst groups of people who have no recent leisure history of trip-making to the countryside need to be better informed about people's motivations, attitudes, preferences and constraints if they are to anticipate any permanent changes in recreational behaviour and environmental awareness. Moreover, the poor quality of life many non-participants have means that promoting and facilitating trips to other destinations such as theme parks or the coast may have greater relative value than trips to Country Parks. 'Helping people help themselves to the countryside' then becomes mis-placed philanthropy. It also leads to the suggestion that the consensus which prevails amongst providers about what countryside recreation actually means is a reflection of middle-class values and attitudes. Countryside recreation – the quiet contemplation of landscape – is somehow deemed to be 'good for people' whether they like it or not.

Conclusion

Numerous initiatives have been taken since the Dart Report of 1976 first drew attention to the role which public transport might play in countryside recreation. They vary from small scale experiments such as Operation Gateway to comprehensive schemes such as that promoted through the Wayfarer Project (Countryside Commission, 1987d). Some have involved the redemption of public transport services which have ceased to operate, such as the many revitalised steam railways that now operate throughout Britain; others have seen the instigation of new services like the mini-bus services which operate in most National Parks. Some services provide new recreational experiences in their own right, for example the pleasure of travelling in the countryside by boat and bicycle. Others are part of a new social experience especially for people who have not visited the countryside recently. Many of the Travel Clubs initiated as part of promoting public transport for recreational purposes fall into this category.

The various initiatives have also differed in terms of their overall objectives. In popular areas such as the National Parks the primary aim has often been to contain car traffic and to manage where visitors go. In others the objective has been to generate new recreational traffic on 'uneconomic' rural routes. Several of the more recent initiatives taken by the urban transport executives have been designed to offer new opportunities for recreational travel to groups of people with special needs, partly by arranging tailor-made trips but also by raising awareness of those opportunities which already exist. It is difficult to draw general conclusions from such a wide range of initiatives, especially in the aftermath of bus deregulation which has brought added difficulties to local authorities and companies wishing to promote integrated schemes for recreational travel across urban boundaries.

There are however a number of common elements to them:

* Most schemes designed to improve awareness of the recreational opportunities in the countryside served by public transport have also involved cheap fares and subsidies. Increases in recreational traffic are thus likely to be a response to both lowered fares and better information.

* Both car owners and non-car owners benefit from most of the schemes. For example, the Sherwood Forester service attracted

133

over 63,000 passenger trips in 1985 and some 40% of the groups visiting the Forest Visitor Centre came from car-owning households. On occasions when cars *are* left at home, 'the environment' may also benefit.

❊ There is some evidence from the Wayfarer project to suggest that both rural and urban residents benefit from comprehensive approaches to promoting recreational routes across the urban boundary. Reciprocal flows between rural and urban areas have increased in some instances.

❊ Most schemes are only as good as the marketing effort invested in them. A professional approach which is targeted to reach particular groups of people and provides clear information about timetables, connecting routes and the activities which can be enjoyed at destinations, has proved effective in maintaining use of recreational travel facilities.

❊ In poor neighbourhoods, better information and travel clubs are unlikely to encourage non-joiners and non-participants to undertake or organise outings to the countryside using public transport. A lack of expertise amongst inhabitants and their unfamiliarity with the countryside and its recreational opportunities means that self-help approaches which are not supported by enthusiastic project workers in the community are not likely to succeed.

❊ Operation Gateway suggests that an 'outreach' approach based on public involvement in recreation as a social service can raise participation levels amongst poor families whereas an approach based on a 'tourism strategy' designed to increase the attractiveness of rural areas through promoting the public transport system, would not. In practice between 1987 and 1989 Operation Gateway became an 'out-reach' or facilitating service funded by the Countryside Commission and latterly by the county council. Designed to inspire interest and enthusiasm both amongst potential users of the countryside and providers, this approach depends critically upon the ability of project officers to make connections between these two groups of people and ultimately to reconcile differences between them about what countryside recreation *means*.

7

Recreation provision and countryside management

....

Introduction

The notion that the countryside requires managing to achieve some desirable land-use outcome is consistent with a planning system which relies on development control as the primary mechanism for guiding land-use change. In rural areas the requirement for manage-ment is made all the more pressing because for the greater part, the landscape of the wider countryside is shaped by the preoccupations of those who own it – private landowners – and by their agricultural and forestry activities which fall outside development control. Earlier chapters have shown that central governments have been reluctant to challenge the proprietorial rights of landowners directly and likewise that county authorities never regarded recreational provision and access to the farmed and settled countryside as a priority in their structure plans, especially amongst those authorities with responsi-bilities for the countryside outside the National Parks (Coalter et al., 1986). Against this background, the decision by the Countryside Commission to initiate several 'countryside management projects' during the 1970s, can be regarded as one measure of the failure of statutory planning mechanisms to protect and provide the kind of countryside and access to it that recreational and environmental inter-ests desired. However, the growing number of such initiatives during the 1980s can also be regarded as a response to central government's insistence on the deregulation of public services, including leisure and highway maintenance services and to the imposition of public expenditure cuts. Under these circumstances, countryside manage-ment offered a pragmatic and conciliatory approach that did not make unreasonable demands on the public purse. In essence however, such approaches are politically motivated because they do not challenge the status quo and for the greater part work outside the statutory planning system.

The range of initiatives embraced by countryside management is wide; some projects are designed to provide multiple land-uses over substantial areas especially in urban-fringe locations and others are designed to promote recreational land use on specific sites and left over pockets of land in the built-up area itself. They are also highly diverse in their approach; some rely heavily on substantial public sector support, whilst others have been able to secure private sector finance and significant practical help in the form of labour from voluntary groups. All are difficult to evaluate without also taking account of the local context in which they have been undertaken and the commitment of the staff engaged in their implementation.

In this chapter three main approaches are examined, namely, Countryside Management, Groundwork Trusts and Community Involvement. The overall objective is to evaluate their success in terms of the following:

※ Have these approaches promoted a variety of outdoor activities and not just those which promote quiet, solitary contemplation of the countryside?

※ When access to land or water is concerned have these approaches secured permanent access arrangements which are participatory rather than exclusionary?

※ Have these approaches promoted access on foot and by public transport rather than by private transport?

※ When new facilities have been provided are these close to disadvantaged neighbourhoods rather than in the more distant locations?

※ Have these initiatives benefited new participants as well as established users?

Countryside management

Towards the end of the 1960s, when the threat of an ever growing wave of recreationists spreading over the countryside was at its height, the Countryside Commission pioneered a new approach to resolving conflicts over access. This approach, called Countryside Management, was first tested in experiments set up in 1969 in the Lake District and in Snowdonia known as the Upland Management

Experiments (UMEX). From the outset, countryside management was conceived as a means of resolving those numerous small scale conflicts that arose between farmers and visitors in the upland areas. Problems such as trespass, vandalism, litter, and footpath maintenance could not be resolved through normal planning solutions but required a more sensitive and flexible approach. This approach called Countryside Management has since come to play an important role in the Commission's approach to other 'problem' areas, for example Heritage coasts (1976) and the urban fringe (1981). In its dependence on a conciliatory approach to resolving conflict and through its use of project officers to effect solutions that are acceptable to all interested parties, countryside management does not address policy conflicts but rather seeks to provide a practical means of resolving the outcome of conflict on the ground. Nevertheless, the approach also anticipates that desirable policy changes will follow if examples of 'good practice' can be demonstrated to work at a low cost (Bromley, 1990).

The success of the approach depends upon the calibre and credibility of the project officers appointed to each Countryside Management Area, particularly upon their ability to act as effective intermediaries between two or more interested parties. The project officer identifies where conflicts arise, brings parties together to discuss constructive ways of resolving them and also organises and implements practical works which may be required on the ground. In the two Upland Management Experiments much of their time was spent in upgrading footpaths and mountain tracks and in addressing problems of access, trespass and vandalism to agricultural property. By liaising directly with private landowners, local authorities and the National Parks Authorities, the project officers achieved a degree of independence of action which allowed them to avoid the delays associated with conventional bureaucratic procedures and by managing a small budget of their own, they were able to implement small-scale works effectively and promptly.

Encouraged by the ability of this approach to resolve small-scale conflicts between farmers and visitors, the Commission extended the approach to the urban-fringe where a greater range of conflicts were identified. It was first used in the Bollin Valley of Manchester in 1972, in an area which had been proposed as a Country Park, but which had been rejected because of landownership problems and antipathy towards the proposal shown by farmers. The pressures of informal recreation on the valley from residents of Manchester's suburbs was great and casual trespass had generated considerable ill-feelings among farmers (Hall, 1976). Some farmers had even erected notices forbidding access and picnicking. At the same time the Valley presented a number of landscape problems which were unlikely to be resolved without the continued existence of viable farming enterprises. Against this background the urban-fringe project aimed to protect farming, create recreation opportunities and protect the landscape from decay. The project officers were given guidelines and terms of reference which allowed them to operate outside the normal framework of local authority activity. Specific tasks were identified and included the following:

* to resolve conflicts (walking v.horse-riding, farming v. recreation);

* to encourage landowners, farmers and public bodies to provide for public access and recreation and to improve the landscape;

* to bring about worthwhile improvements in landscape and access by using small sums of money allocated for the purpose;

* to take action to remove eyesores and reduce the impact of litter and vandalism;

* to make maximum use of voluntary effort to carry out tasks.

The project was staffed by a full-time officer, a full-time ranger who organised estate management work and three part-time rangers (retired men) with duties that included providing information and patrolling. No project was undertaken in the valley that cost more than £300. The experience of this and other countryside management projects has shown that to be effective, a project officer requires an initial period of orientation in which to acquire local knowledge and to develop contacts with local interests. These time-consuming activities mean that work on the ground starts some time after the officer is first appointed and, depending on the life of the management project, these delays may mean that the officer cannot devote much time to an overall assessment of how the area can be improved. It was with this broader objective in mind that later schemes incorporated the preparation and adoption of area management plans as an integral part of the project's objectives. As Elson (1986) demonstrates, central government has resisted attempts to promote statutory land-use plans for extensive areas such as green belts but, the adoption of small-area management plans by local and county authorities as part of their indicative planning activities has found acceptance. The plans however, do not have any statutory status and are expressions of intent to pursue desirable land-use outcomes by the participating authorities rather than legally binding obligations. Hence they are vulnerable to changes in the priorities and commitment of participating parties.

In successive urban-fringe experiments in Hertfordshire and Havering in London, and elsewhere, the combination of the project officer and the preparation and adoption of a Management Plan by those planning authorities involved in these areas, has proved to be one means of ensuring that the multiple problems of urban-fringe areas are given specific attention. But in practice, project officers have found it easier to resolve specific conflicts than to influence the policies of individual landowners, organizations or public agencies. Often the underlying causes of conflict such as extensive dereliction cannot be resolved within the short-timescale of the projects and the varying political commitment of all the public authorities means that a comprehensive approach to countryside management is often prevented. Importantly too, the prevailing 'ideology' of what recreational use of the urban-fringe is appropriate, serves to constrain the range of innovative recreational uses that have been pursued. A survey of the recreational potential of London's Green Belt completed on behalf of the Sports Council and the Countryside Commission (1986) for example reinforces these points and highlights in particular the case of motor sports (See also Sports Council and Countryside Commission, 1990b).

The achievements of countryside management

In their assessment of the Urban Fringe Management Experiments (Countryside Commission, 1985) consultants pointed to the successes and limitations of countryside management. In particular they pointed to the limited success such an approach has in coping with the legacy of substantial environmental dereliction. When dereliction is extensive and arises through major structural changes in the national and local economy, as for example was the case in the London Borough of Havering, the UFEX approach appears as little more than a cosmetic exercise. Under these conditions it proved difficult to get different land agencies and local authorities together to fund a comprehensive approach to environmental improvement.

Their experiences also suggested that many projects were attempts to compensate for poor levels of provision that were properly the responsibility of the local authority or the land owner, as for example was the case with poor levels of recreation provision in some public housing estates and the poor condition of public Rights of Way over farmland (Figure 7.1). Furthermore, the report records a considerable degree of frustration amongst project officers and the Commission's central and regional staff because county and local authorities failed to pursue landscaping schemes in their overall policies, whilst private owners benefited substantially from planting schemes and other grants sponsored by the Commission. In this respect, the Commission's

Figure 7.1: Havering urban fringe Countryside Management area
Source: Countryside Commission, 1982

Table 7.1: Summary of completed tasks in Hertfordshire Countryside Management Area
Source: Countryside Commission, 1982

Task	Number of projects
Stiles/bridges/fences/gates	65
Scrub clearance	33
Tree planting and maintenance	28
Tree felling and surgery	12
Rubbish clearance	10
Bridleway: ditching/grading/surfacing	9
Woodland management	5
Nature conservation	5
Recreation play areas	2
Education	4
Total	**173**

expectation that public authorities would 'set the example' for other land-owners proved to be overly optimistic, predictably some local authorities proved to be more responsive than others.

One of the major benefits the report points to is the success Countryside Management Areas have had at focusing attention on the countryside which straddles administrative boundaries. In London for example, the borough of Barnet adopted a comprehensive approach to landscaping and land management together with Hertfordshire County Council. Recently too, similar benefits have arisen from cross-boundary initiatives taken in the West Dorset Countryside Management Area. In these cases, the role of the project officer as entrepreneur and facilitator proved to be an effective one both at an administrative and planning level. Moreover, by up-grading footpaths, promoting cross-boundary public transport links and constructing new bridleways, bridges, stiles and the like, new access opportunities were secured to tracts of countryside which previously would not have received attention (Table 7.1). Such small-scale achievements are the hall mark of the Countryside Management approach and together with its ability to involve local volunteers and the local community in the practical implementation of these activities recommend it as a low-cost approach (Probert and Hamersley, 1978).

Overall this approach to countryside management brings modest success. For example, some improvements can be made to specific landscape components through introducing more trees, hedges and ponds but the approach has little influence on the way farmers farm or on the overall environmental policies of local authorities and other public agencies. Improvements in access can be achieved, but these are often restricted to existing public Rights of Way and when new routes are negotiated, they are often secured on a permissive basis and can be terminated by either party at short notice. Likewise, improvements to existing recreation sites often favour car-based recreation rather than focusing attention on other forms of vehicular use such as motorcycles or trail bikes and, by improving facilities at existing sites rather than on sites accessible on foot and close to residential areas, few genuinely *new* recreational opportunities are achieved. Importantly too, a 'tidying-up' approach that results from an emphasis on small projects rather than strategic issues may also lead to the loss of informal, adventure areas used for 'illicit' play or activities such as motorbike scrambling and the like. As a result some sections of the local community benefit at the expense of others. Furthermore, as Elson (1986) points out, once the Countryside Management Service becomes incorporated into the activities of the county council, as is the case in Hertfordshire, it becomes an instrument of public policy rather than a mechanism for resolving land-use conflicts among different constituencies of users, as was the original intention.

It was against this background of 'modest success', that in 1980 the Commission launched a new, 'extensive' Urban Fringe Experiment in the form of Operation Groundwork based on St. Helens and Knowsley (Figure 7.2). By 1985 the approach pioneered in the North West had became a national venture – The Groundwork Foundation (Groundwork Foundation, 1986).

The Groundwork Trusts

From the outset the Groundwork approach was heralded as a new approach because it aimed to establish a local partnership between private, public and voluntary sectors. Using the experience gained from the first Groundwork Trust established in the St Helens area, each Trust is constituted as a limited company with charitable status and is governed by a board of trustees drawn from representatives of local authorities, local businesses and environmental or voluntary interests. Commonly, each board involves some ten to twelve people who meet quarterly, with the day-to-day running of the company carried out by a full-time director and a small group of four to five full-time assistants. The main function of this team is to play an enabling and catalytic role in bringing people and resources together in pursuit of a common cause. Through their administration by a board with broadly based interests, their constitution as a 'third force' which is neither public nor private, and through their expertise in environmental management, the Trusts are promoted as being able to make a unique contribution to clearing up the environmental legacy of

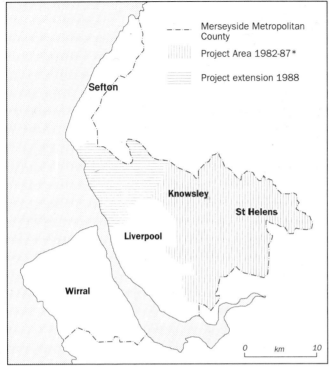

*at the outset the urban areas of Knowsley were excluded

Figure 7.2: St Helens and Knowsley Project area
Source: Groundwork Foundation, 1989

industrial dereliction in the urban fringe and, increasingly, to urban regeneration (Groundwork Foundation, 1986). By concentrating their efforts on putting wasteland to good use the Trusts make use of the Derelict Land Grant administered by the Department of the Environment and by providing land management services to the public and private sector, they are able to generate their own income as well. At the outset, the trusts gained up to a third of their funding from central government; first by employing people on Community Programme schemes funded through the Manpower Services Commission (MSC) and later from the Department of the Environment; second by benefiting from core funding from the Countryside Commission and later through the Urban Programme; and most recently by seemingly gaining preferential access to Department of Environment funds such as the Derelict Land Grant (Collis, 1990).

143

In practice the projects completed by each Trust vary in character, funding and man-power resourcing. These differences reflect the personalities involved, local environmental conditions and the extent to which each Trust seeks to involve the local community. Annual reports of the Trusts illustrate the range of projects undertaken. For example in 1984–5, the projects budget of £25,000 for the St. Helens and Knowsley Trust generated a programme of 54 projects to the value of £370,000 on the ground (Groundwork Trust Annual Report). By contrast, the Rochdale and Oldham Groundwork put more effort into promoting voluntary involvement and had not been able to secure MSC approval for any of its schemes although 5,000 days of work from volunteers, community groups and schoolchildren were generated on Local Groundwork schemes in 1985.

Within the range of environmental improvements undertaken by the Groundwork Trusts only a limited number have been directed to upgrading recreational facilities, improving access to them and to providing information about walks and similar activities. Figure 7.3 illustrates the priority given to problems identified by members of the St. Helens Trust and serves to emphasize that priority is given to environmental improvement rather than to other kinds of projects. Nevertheless some projects have been directed towards improving recreational facilities. For example, two projects undertaken by Groundwork Macclesfield have provided a popular greenway along the route of the old Macclesfield to Marple railway and a cycle-hire scheme makes use of this traffic-free route. The towpath along the Macclesfield canal has also been improved and provides a parallel route linking town and country.

Overall, few trusts have taken an active and promotional role with respect to recreation although the Rossendale Trust is an exception. This Trust has extended its remit with respect to recreation by establishing a forum – Access Rossendale – which attempts to reconcile and resolve conflicting recreational interests at the local level. The forum brings together representatives from organizations involved with recreation, conservation, amenity and local community groups with the objective of establishing an 'access consensus'. The group then acts as an access lobby and presses its claims on the local authority. The Groundwork Trust may then act as the agent of the local authority to carry out the practical tasks generated by these claims. To date, this approach has involved a survey of the condition of Rights of Way in the local area and improvements to them rather than the pursuit of new initiatives designed to secure and extend access. The access lobby is thus a means of persuading the local authority and local land owners to fulfill their statutory obligations over Rights of Way.

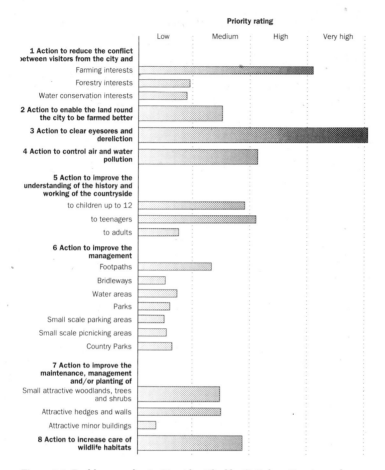

Figure 7.3: Problems and priorities identified by St Helens Trust members
Source: Groundwork Foundation, 1989

The extent to which the forum can act as a means of securing *new* access arrangements for less conventional recreational activities, remains to be seen. The Access Study (Countryside Commission, 1987) suggests that such a forum, working with the Groundwork Trust, offers a possible model for a 'clearer definition of (and possible solution to) some access issues' (p.116). The report acknowledges however, that while the forum provides a means of achieving collaboration among different organizations, it may also serve to buffer the local authority from the real weight of local community pressures. It may also serve to build up expectations for action amongst its members when the local authority is reluctant to act, either because it lacks resources or commitment.

The establishment of the Groundwork Foundation as a national organization in 1985 which aims to expand the Groundwork movement into the older, run-down industrial areas where there is under-used land, buildings and labour, marks a growing commitment to this partnership approach. The first task for the Foundation was to secure increased resources for all the local trusts viewed with dismay the potential withdrawal of core-funding and the expectation that they should be self-financing. The report of the Foundation's property panel (Groundwork Foundation, 1986),made it clear that many trusts would not be able to survive without core-funding. This report examined potential sources of funding for the Trusts and pointed to the limited amounts donated by the private sector – the total level of charitable donations given by companies in Britain is very small, (about 0.2% of gross profit or about £70 million on average a year). The panel suggested that Trusts could benefit from increases in the derelict land grant and through those management grants anticipated by the DOE to provide core funding for voluntary bodies which play a regional role in this regard. This latter role was deemed to be especially important in the absence of the considerable support given to the Trusts by the former Metropolitan Counties and in the light of changing policies for employment training through which the trusts had benefited in their early years. Without core funding, rolling programmes of environmental upgrading and recreation provision could not be entertained and projects would only be initiated on a piece-meal basis. Faced with the enormous problems of land dereliction encountered in many northern cities, such piece-meal projects amount to little more than the environmental cosmetics identified by the Countryside Commission in its earlier management experiments.

In the short term the property panel of the Groundwork Foundation recommended that the Trusts focus on setting up projects that local people will value so that Trusts can win the support of the local authorities in particular. The Foundation clearly expects the Trusts to perform a public service which neither duplicates the services provided by the local authorities nor deflects public agencies and other individuals from carrying out their responsibilities. Given sufficient managerial and manpower resources and financed from sources that do not compete with those required by the local authorities for other services, the Trusts might be able to achieve the low-cost 'ruralisation' of urban areas and their fringes envisaged by the directors. Unless however, there is an obvious mechanism for incorporating the work of the Trusts into the local planning process, the Trusts run the risk of compensating for the failure of the local authorities and other public agencies from carrying out their responsibilities in much the same way that earlier experiments in Countryside Management had identified. Furthermore, an emphasis on setting up projects local people will value, could imply an approach based on 'marketing a product' rather than one necessarily based on communal values. In this case it is not immediately clear whether the Groundwork approach is any more effective than any other for assessing what local communities want. Neither is it clear which constituencies amongst local communities will benefit most – private business interests or local residents.

Over the short life of the Groundwork Trusts these partnerships have achieved a limited measure of success in promoting an approach to environmental improvement which has encouraged the public sector, including local authorities, to fund new projects when formerly they did not (Boaden, 1989). The extent to which the Trusts can build on this momentum and can change attitudes will not only depend upon the continued support from central government funding, but will also depend upon their ability to persuade local communities to undertake a long term commitment to managing the new environments they have helped to create. Without this commitment, the greening of the city's countryside the Trusts have initiated will amount to little more than a new form of environmental dereliction. How to involve local communities in the creation and after-care of these new landscapes, especially those with no obvious leisure function, is a question that needs answering if these new landscapes and the new recreational experiences they purport to provide, are not to deteriorate. The solution apparently favoured by existing Trusts, is to set up a trading arm to act as a land management consultancy. Any profits so generated, are then reinvested into other non-profit making projects. In this sense revenue is raised but unless committed staff are prepared to research and discover what local people want, as well as what businesses are prepared to pay for, it is difficult to see how communities as a whole benefit from this approach. In the final analysis, it is by investing in human resources rather than the approach itself which is likely to prove the key to success. On this point, the experience of other initiatives in community involvement is instructive.

Community involvement and recreational need

1981 saw the publication of a study by Dower and his colleagues which represented the outcome of an extended project on *Leisure Provision and People's Needs* (Dower et al. 1981). The project, which

147

had made a detailed study of leisure provision in the London borough of Brent incorporated extended interviews with a wide-cross section of the community, household surveys and detailed analyses of leisure provision across a broad field of leisure pursuits. It was a comprehensive attempt to explore the mismatch between people's leisure requirements and the facilities and resources available to them through the public sector. The main recommendation of the report was that a better matching of people's leisure needs would be provided by an approach to provision based on community involvement rather than on one which continued to rely on a traditional 'standards' approach used by most local authorities.

Written at a time of growing economic recession, the report was quick to point out that financial stringency is a double-edged sword – 'drying up some sources of support but also stimulating the search for "small things that make big differences".' (Dower et al. 1981, p.7.) They saw community involvement as a way of both meeting people's needs and increasing a community's resourcefulness. However, as Limb's (1986) study shows, community involvement in leisure provision can be used to achieve political as well as practical objectives and it is not the 'politically-neutral' approach its name suggests.

Limb's study undertaken in an urban-fringe borough in London – Hillingdon, followed the course of community involvement initiatives in open-space provision over a ten-year period during which the borough changed its political allegiance. Over this time three forms of community involvement were pursued. These included conservation projects designed to improve open spaces, joint committees to advise on the management of open space, and devolution of the management of facilities to clubs and organizations. Through a detailed analysis of the origin of some 40 projects, the mechanisms used to implement them and the social status of community participants, Limb identified three forms of community involvement in the borough. First, a number of small-scale co-operative projects owed their existence to the personal enthusiasm of a single officer. Second, three projects involved the establishment of a 'working party' which involved local officers, councillors and residents, set up primarily as a defence mechanism on the part of the local authority in order to deflect criticism of their actions. Third, devolution of management of a number of facilities, such as community halls and allotments had been pursued originally by the Labour council in order to save money and to increase public participation and later by the Conservatives in furtherance of their desire to encourage private enterprise.

Limb's study suggests that there are formidable barriers which prevent lower socio-economic groups from participating in these forms of community involvement. They include poor knowledge of the lines of communication used by elected representatives of the council to detect need, especially the importance of social networks. Reliance of the local authority on organised groups within the community to represent legitimate interests and their reluctance to discuss complaints with ad-hoc groups also proved a problem. Officers often regarded community involvement as a threat to their professional status, especially when community dissatisfaction was interpreted as a challenge to their expertise. Such a challenge provoked defensive responses on behalf of the officers and resulted in off-putting rebuttals to complainants. Lastly, councillors in Hillingdon regarded the question of financial accountability as a problem in communities where local residents did not possess professional qualifications such as those of accountancy, business management and organizational skills. Under these circumstances only the higher status groups in the community are likely to be regarded as acceptable participants in community involvement. Operated in this way, community involvement serves to preserve the status-quo by identifying and listening to 'legitimate users' only, much as the Access Study describes for 'appropriate' recreational uses in the wider countryside.

Limb concludes that any attempt to make participation in outdoor leisure provision and management more socially equitable would require an approach which invested in more support staff and made more funds available to them. In addition, a change in attitudes of councillors and officers to the resourcefulness and legitimacy of claims made by lower status groups in society would be required. Were community groups to be assisted through an outreach approach, community involvement would then be akin to community development and leisure provision could be placed on a par alongside education, housing and health as the social service the White Paper of 1975 urged. In the forms practiced by most local authorities, as Limb's wider study of all London boroughs revealed (Limb, 1986b), community involvement in leisure provision is a political and practical expediency which tends to benefit those who were already well served and which leaves questions of equity and equality of opportunity, unaddressed.

Limb's study did not attempt to determine the extent to which communities become more resourceful and perhaps acquired new skills in the process of participation in community projects. This kind of evaluation is linked with notions of leisure as life-enhancement. Such evaluations are difficult to make because the benefits of community involvement are largely intangible and difficult to demonstrate other than through qualitative assessments. But such intangible benefits may outweigh any measurable improvements in increased provision or access to facilities. Mostyn's study (1979), undertaken for the Nature Conservancy Council, used once-only discussion groups with people who had participated in wildlife conservation projects on open spaces, to explore these kinds of benefits. Participants mentioned a wide range of personal benefits – emotional benefits, intellectual ones – including the learning of new 'country skills'; social benefits that accrue from working in a team as well as the physical pleasures derived from physical exertion and 'mucking about'. For some people too, involvement had a long-term influence on their education and career choice. Without longitudinal studies of people's experiences and career development it is difficult to determine the full extent of these benefits amongst the community as a whole but, such studies do point to the very real ways in which community involvement in outdoor activities can be life-enhancing.

As well as identifying benefits of participation Mostyn's study also revealed a number of frustrations which depressed and discouraged participants. Vandalism, rubbish dumping and litter were the most frustrating, and the lack of care and concern shown by the local authorities meant that many people felt discouraged about the future of the site they had worked on because they did not trust the authorities. In this sense the after-care of open-spaces, amenity areas, nature parks and wildlife sites presents a particular problem for these areas require a continuing commitment if sites are not to deteriorate. When local authorities encourage or at least condone community initiatives for site improvement but are not themselves prepared to provide the continuing after-care that is required, this burden falls on the local community. Bradley's study (1986) demonstrates that many local communities are not in a position to provide the high standards of management such areas require and in the absence of management these new amenity landscapes soon appear uncared for and derelict. Initiatives are then mocked and derided and the whole basis of the 'greening movement' and justification for community involvement is soon called into question. Underlying Bradley's study therefore, is an attempt to identify how high standards of after-care can be achieved in urban and urban-fringe locations where there is no tradition of countryside or amenity land management.

Drawing on a comparison between rural and urban environments, the report shows how the British Trust for Conservation Volunteers (BTCV) has provided a pivotal role in providing after-care on sites in the rural area. The BTCV provides volunteer workers, professional supervisors and advisers and the tools required for a wide range of environmental tasks. The trust is organised on a local and regional basis but many of the volunteers are drawn from the urban area. In practice, whilst the number of tasks performed in the rural area dominates their work schedule, many are also undertaken in the urban fringe. As a result the BTCV has built up considerable expertise in both the management of naturalistic areas and in the creation of new amenity habitats.

Within the urban area itself, public open spaces are managed by the local authorities through their Leisure Services Department or equivalent. Volunteers like the BTCV, seeking to establish a role for themselves in creating and managing open spaces in the urban area find themselves 'competing' with these professional staff much as Limb describes (1986a). In many circumstances local authority staff are over stretched and additional tasks which do not fit readily into existing work schedules cannot be accommodated. As a result, the burden of after-care of sites which have been designed and established using volunteers and members of the local community with the blessing of the local authority, falls on the community.

Bradley and others have shown (Laurie 1987, Bradshaw, Goode and Thorp, 1986) that even in authorities where these new green landscapes are incorporated into existing public open spaces, the expertise of parks staff in providing the quality of environmental management required by naturalistic areas is restricted. Many members of parks departments have been trained in a tradition of groundsmanship and horticulture, not ecology and amenity land management. In addition, inflexible approaches to site management are reinforced by a system of funding which favours capital expenditure not maintenance expenditure, and by staffing arrangements which favour standardized tasks and not specialized care that is sensitive to the ecological conditions of a site or the recreational needs of the local community as Limb has shown. Competitive tendering and contracting of leisure services in local authorities can be expected to reinforce this standardization process especially in the absence of informed professionals responsible for drawing up the contracts in the first place.

Based on her study of over 40 case studies of community greening, ranging from community gardens and allotments to housing co-operatives and natural parks, Bradley concludes, that additional skills are required by parks staff, if the after-care of more naturalistic open-spaces is to remain the responsibility of the local authority. In cases where a more ecologically sensitive approach is required for example in coppicing, hedge laying, pond maintenance etc. the skills offered by voluntary organizations such as BTCV may be called upon. At present however, because the number of ecologists and landscape architects employed in Leisure Services Departments who might serve as the contact between local authorities, the community and volunteers is so small, little progress is likely to be made in promoting new approaches to after-care. Bradley suggests that the role played by the task organiser as someone who both assembles a team of volunteers and the equipment appropriate for the task, and as the individual with whom the commissioning agency or owner of the site liaises about the nature of the task itself, is a key one.

In the rural area this key role is generally played by the supervisory staff of BTCV who advise and liaise directly with the land owner, In the case of the urban area, such an individual would have a tripartite role to play. First the key person would need to liaise between the various departments of the local authority itself – housing, estates, parks, planning and leisure services. Second they would need to liaise between the local authority or land owner and the local community, and third between the authority/owner and the volunteer workforce. Such a person would require good communication skills as well as a sound training in the design and management of amenity areas. Critically however, they would also require support from specialist out-reach staff who can spend time understanding and articulating what local people regard as important. In practice therefore, as is the case with the Groundwork trusts, it is the number and calibre of staff that is likely to secure success for such an approach and not necessarily the merits of the approach itself.

The preferred solution Bradley suggests is one that fits with the Groundwork Trust approach. She advocates the appointment of key-people who are able to perform this tripartite role but, she also regards the continuing commitment on behalf of the local authority to perform the routine tasks of management as an important requirement. Her survey suggests that many community groups found the burden of after-care intolerable especially as far as routine tasks were concerned because they provided little satisfaction either to volunteers or to members of the local community. In the absence of key personnel who may be able to make routine task more satisfying through organizing events and by stimulating participation in the manner of 'animateurs', Bradley suggests that community commitment to performing routine maintenance tasks will wane over time. Precisely because much of the motivation for involvement stems from participating in novel and creative tasks associated with the design and construction of site facilities and habitats, and not from the routine and undemanding tasks associated with after-care, such as litter-collection, grass cutting and fence repair, community involvement in greening cannot be sustained without an *equal* partnership between the local authorities and the community and volunteers. The implication is that the Groundwork Trusts can provide the mechanism for forging this new approach to amenity landscapes and that members of their staff can provide the key-personnel required to serve as managing agents and animateurs. But the role of the public sector is also a crucial one particularly in the providing a permanency of commitment that the Trust approach as yet, cannot provide. In which case the question arises – couldn't the same role be played by a revitalized and well-resourced local authority?

Conclusion

The range of approaches to land management discussed in this chapter are essentially conciliatory in style and often operate outside the statutory planning system. For these reasons alone they raise important questions about the role of the public sector. In essence, the role of Countryside Management projects, Groundwork trusts and community involvement in helping to provide living landscapes which also function effectively as recreational environments is designed to compliment that provided by the public sector and not to replace it. If this is the case then these new approaches may well create innovatory provision that is more effective than traditional approaches in meeting people's recreational needs. But, as Limb's study has shown, such approaches are not the politically-neutral approach they appear to be and the extent to which all sections of the community benefit from them, is not self- evident. Also clear is the fact that local authorities are not the equal partners the Groundwork Trusts suggest (Collis, 1990). Rather, by having access to special funding administered by central government through the DOE, the Trusts can by-pass local authorities. Of perhaps greater significance however, is the fact that the Groundwork approach is pragmatic and ad hoc and does not address the causes of the profound social and environmental problems their activities are designed to ease. That there are now over 23 Groundwork Trusts is confirmation that these problems are widespread and common but, a pragmatic approach assists some people in some areas and not others and favours certain kinds of provision and not others. Moreover, major strategic issues of landownership, resource allocation, accessibility and communal values are not addressed.

Like Countryside Management before and many projects which purport to 'involve the community', the Groundwork Trusts are conciliatory in approach and politically-inspired. In the final analysis such approaches are not rooted in a desire to promote outdoor leisure activities as life-enhancing or to promote community development, but in a desire to get things done even if it means marginalizing local authorities and the constituencies they are accountable to in the process. For these reasons it will be instructive to monitor how successful recent initiatives taken by the Countryside Commission and the Forestry Commission (1989) to create several new 'Community Forests' will be at identifying and providing the range of recreational experiences local people desire.

8

Countryside recreation in contemporary society
....

The main purpose of this book has been to show how the countryside
aesthetic has come to occupy a dominant position in public debates
about the recreational use of the countryside. Owing much to the centrality of property rights in British society and the laws and customs
associated with them, the countryside aesthetic has been used by
landed interests to determine where, what and when people can enjoy
the countryside. In this way, productive uses of the countryside such
as agriculture and forestry have been protected at the expense of recreational and leisure uses. As a result, citizens in England and Wales do
not enjoy the 'freedom to roam' like many of their European neighbours and several recreational activities and outdoor pursuits have
not been able to 'find a place' in the countryside.

Intervention by the public sector in countryside recreation in the post-
war period has brought only marginal improvements in access to the
wider countryside and in the extent to which a range of outdoor pursuits can be undertaken in an informal way in the countryside. 'Non-
rural' pursuits such as motor-cross, trail and mountain biking for
example still find it difficult to secure access to the countryside and a
variety of water-based activities are constrained in a similar way. Not
only has public intervention been limited and circumscribed by the
supremacy of proprietorial rights but, the form intervention has taken
has also been constrained by the prevailing view held by professionals in planning and leisure services through which countryside recreation is portrayed as 'the quiet enjoyment of open country'. Enshrined
in the National Parks Act of 1949, this form of enjoyment has become
the *only* acceptable way of enjoying the wider countryside as well as
those outstanding areas the Act was designed to conserve. In
consequence, public sector involvement in countryside recreation
has become dominated by a site-based policy of low-key provision in
which sites are deliberately set aside and managed for 'quiet
enjoyment'.

Expressing the social basis upon which this policy is founded, Newby (1988), likened these areas to 'environmental Bantustans' and thereby highlighted how strong the alliance between private landed interests and rural planning authorities in particular had become. Sharing with landowners a reluctance to accept that the countryside and its enjoyment is socially and culturally constructed, planners reinforced this ideology by resorting to the use of supposedly value-free concepts such as carrying-capacity and gravity-models to defend and implement a site-based policy. Even when in the 1970s, the national government of the day and the national agency responsible for countryside recreation sought to pursue socially-motivated policies, the strength of this alliance ensured that the status quo prevailed and the interests of several outdoor activities were never addressed. Today this same concept of carrying capacity underpins the consultation paper 'A Countryside for Sport' prepared by the Sports Council (1990) as part of its policy review of sport and recreation in the countryside.

Such an analysis suggests that as long as proprietorial rights remain so central to the way society is organized, and the attitudes and values of rural planning authorities serve to reinforce the countryside aesthetic, public debates about the future recreational role of the countryside will continue to be framed and dominated by this ideology. But there are also signs that this status quo is being contested. The changing economic fortunes of rural areas and the changing social composition of rural constituencies, coupled with a heightened awareness of environmental issues amongst the general public, means that attitudes to the countryside and its use are changing in unpredictable ways. This chapter now turns to a consideration of whether these changes are likely to forge new alliances amongst interests previously disposed towards the protection of the countryside aesthetic.

The chapter examines relationships between socio-economic change and leisure demands on the countryside by drawing on structural theories of social change and leisure culture. These theories suggest that critical to the way in which new recreational and leisure demands will be accommodated in the countryside is the extent to which there is a general willingness in society to accept market mechanisms as the correct means of gaining access to the countryside and a willingness amongst participants in outdoor recreation to become organized through clubs and membership groups before they can enjoy access to the countryside. Without this general acceptance, there may well be new calls for selective legislation to open up the wider countryside for informal leisure uses.

The chapter also looks at the extent to which changes in the economy and planning system might contribute to a reassessment of the productive activities of landowners and to changes in their attitudes towards the leisure use of the countryside. It explores briefly how recent changes in the agricultural sector, linked with a liberalization of the planning system, have begun to erode the homogeneity of values held by rural landowners towards recreational uses of the countryside. Through this process of reassessment, landed interests may find it more profitable and practical to promote leisure uses of rural land than in the past and as a result some leisure activities may find it easier to negotiate access to the countryside than they did. In the light of these broad changes, the chapter turns finally to a consideration of the role the public sector might play in countryside recreation in the future.

Leisure culture in contemporary society

Commentators on contemporary society point to several ways in which society differs from its predecessors (Urry, 1988, Thrift and Williams, 1987). Notable is the changing basis of employment structure where a decline in manufacturing industries and a rise in service industries has benefited a skilled-work force but has provided fewer employment opportunities for unskilled people. Viewed in this framework, the rise of a 'service class' within the social division of labour is a reflection of broad, structural changes in the economy of many western nations. Members of a 'service class' are well educated and possess the necessary credentials for good career prospects. Furthermore, the occupations they hold are not principally involved with the ownership of capital but with institutions that service it – occupations in information technology, training and marketing, investment, banking and insurance. Urry (1988) suggests that a service class comprises 'a powerful yet relatively unanchored social grouping which has begun to impose its framework upon much of wider society, and hence its distinctions of taste have become highly significant for other classes and social groups' (p.41, 1988). Following this line of argument the leisure culture favoured by these social groupings might be expected to have an important effect on the way in which the countryside is defined and used for leisure pursuits.

Urry points to several ways in which the tastes of a service class impinge on the significance attributed to the countryside and its enjoyment and protection. First 'culture' is prioritized and through the conscious acquisition of good taste, members of a service class come to share middle-class values which hold the aesthetic tradition of the countryside in high esteem. In this way the pastoral idyll of the post-enclosure landscape is revered – the countryside aesthetic – but, scant attention is paid to the conditions of rural society which support it. Second, to live in the countryside also becomes a goal for people who have benefited from the rise of service industries, and for many of them this goal has been achieved (Thrift and Williams, 1987). Third, the arrival of these new residents in established rural communities however, can provoke a clash of cultures because motivational and attitudinal divisions also occur within leisure culture itself. Urry cites an array of cultural symbols and leisure pursuits which are interpreted as the subversion of the 'rituals of the bourgeois order' (p.42) by a service class, including health foods, real ale, antiques and old houses and a general dislike of organized leisure. Jogging, swimming, cycling, walking, fly-fishing, wind-surfing and mountaineering are enjoyed both because they are uncontrived but, also because they contribute to a sense of self-development, excitement and adventure. In other words, participation in a range of outdoor pursuits is not motivated primarily by a desire to be supportive of, or accepted by, the established social order but, by a new set of ideals and goals.

As long as new participants engage in 'quasi-rural' sports and place little demands on the countryside save access on foot or horseback, new leisure demands do not offend the countryside aesthetic and do not present themselves as a challenge to the status quo. On the other hand, the scope for conflict is heightened when this aesthetic is challenged by noisy activities and non-rural sports and by recreationalists who refuse to be organized. Moreover, if landowners do not permit access to the leisure environments people have so recently moved to in the expectation that they can be enjoyed, conflict is also likely to arise. Paradoxically though, as the Access Study suggests, some 'new residents' are often more vocal in their protection of the countryside ideal than established residents and it is new residents, un-tutored in the ways of the countryside but vociferous in the protection of their newly acquired 'rights', who farmers and rural landowners regard as most problematic. Hence, it is difficult to predict what role the countryside aesthetic will play in determining the future leisure use of the countryside because it is not clear whether members of a service class will defend or contest it. It is clear however, that members of a service class are likely to play an important role in the resolution of land-use conflicts, particularly when these new residents become involved directly in the institutions responsible for planning and protecting the countryside they have worked hard to secure and enjoy.

In practice, both because the growth in rural settlements has been uneven and because the attitudes and values of new residents are not homogeneous, the outcomes of particular contests are likely to be spatially uneven. Critical to the resolution of conflicts relating to the leisure use of the countryside however, will be the attitudes of a service class to proprietorial rights as a basis for securing recreational access to land and water and their willingness to become organized in clubs and groups through which their access demands can be pursued. Without general support for both of these mechanisms, the 'countryside aesthetic' is likely to be challenged, not least because the motives of a service class for engaging in a variety of leisure pursuits are different and because, as Urry suggests, they transgress cultural norms.

In essence, it is through their readiness to transgress the cultural norms of 'group' whether this be age-group, gender, race, class or neighbourhood, that a service class impinges most dramatically on leisure culture. This 'decentering' of identity has many expressions, for example in the transgression of boundaries through play, the casting on and off of identities and the opportunities to engage vicariously in other people's lives. Theme parks, medieval fayres and feasts, pop festivals and 'living' museums provide the opportunities to temporarily adopt identities which have new meanings for their participants. As part of postmodernism this dismemberment of group norms allows people to lead eclectic lives 'unshackled by the legacy of tradition or collective expectation' and to respond freely to the market place. But in turn, these consumers are fickle in their loyalties and demand is less easy to satisfy or predict. In this way 'elite' sports such as polo, target archery, shooting, fly-fishing, ballooning and flying can expect to be penetrated by new participants drawn from amongst a service class but, in what numbers and when is less easily determined. Likewise new outdoor activities such as war-games marketed as 'Skirmish' and 'Combat' are a means of packaging an activity which otherwise could only be engaged in by conforming to establishment norms. The extent to which rural communities at large and planning committees in particular will accept this form of recreation as an 'appropriate' one for a countryside location is also less easily determined, although the liberalization of the planning system itself has made it easier for new leisure uses to legitimize their claims for inclusion in the countryside.

If this kind of structural analysis is correct in its diagnosis that a service class is likely to imprint its leisure values and tastes on the rest of society, then new forms of rural tourism and quasi-rural sports will make new demands on the countryside and will present challenges to the countryside aesthetic on several fronts. The demand for leisure complexes in National Parks and green belt locations is just one indication of this challenge and others are likely to follow. How they will be reconciled however will apparently depend increasingly upon the individual circumstances of each case. The devolution of planning responsibilities to local authorities noted by Munton (1983) and Elson (1986) and the variable response this has provoked to similar development applications, means that the outcomes themselves will be unpredictable and individualistic. Moreover, changes in General Development Orders and Use Class Orders made during the 1980s have meant that certain leisure uses are exempt from planning control when previously they were not. Coming a time when public subsidies are being withdrawn from agriculture and are being redirected to environmentally sensitive land-uses, such changes mean that leisure uses of rural land have gained a new significance as a source of income.

In the process of reassessing their capital assets, landlords can turn to leisure uses of their land as means of raising their incomes and these changes in the planning system have made it easier for landowners to promote these kind of uses. Home (1987) suggests that the leisure industry now has the same freedom from control as agriculture and hence landowners are likely to take advantage of their new-found freedom. Camping, caravanning, amusement parks and leisure domes are just some of the leisure uses that might follow from these changes. Coupled with a general increase in demand for outdoor leisure activities, the liberalization of the planning system means that the countryside aesthetic will be challenged from a broad range of interests. Furthermore, it is likely that the traditional alliance between landowners, conservation and amenity groups and the planning profession will be eroded both by landowners seeking to realize their landed assets and by new residents seeking new leisure experiences.

What role the countryside aesthetic will play in the mediation of conflict remains problematic because other evidence suggests that a heightened public awareness of environmental issues means that the number of people who seek to conserve the countryside for 'its own sake' has also grown – among them, members of a service class (Lowe and Flyn, 1989 and Miller and Tranter, 1988). Social change in these terms suggests that there are many more people in society who are both protectors and users of the countryside (Figure 8.1) and this duality is expressed most potently through what enjoying the countryside has now come to mean for landowners, new rural residents and potential visitors to the countryside.

This kind of analysis of modern social and cultural values suggests that employment opportunities are the root cause of changing attitudes to countryside recreation although changes in the economic and planning context within which landlords and local authorities are making decisions about new land uses is also important. Recent

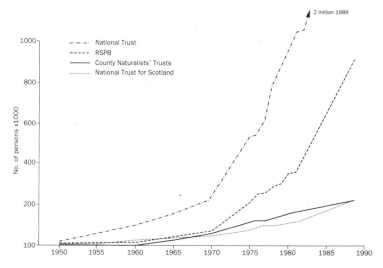

Figure 8.1: Membership of major environmental groups
Source: Digest of Countryside Recreation Statistics 1978. Countryside
Commission and updated figures from relevant bodies

evidence from the Social Attitudes survey of 1987 and 1990 provides
some support for this interpretation and it also suggests that public
attitudes to the countryside and its appropriate use are changing
(Young, 1989 and 1990).

Changing social attitudes

One of the objectives of the British Social Attitude Survey is to explore
people's attitudes to the countryside and its future. In summarising
responses to questions about the countryside, Young suggests that
there has been a dramatic trend in the proportion of people expressing
strong concern about countryside changes between 1985 and 1987
(Table 8.1). Although people in Social Classes I and II register much
higher levels of concern than other classes, heightened concern is universal and of similar magnitude in all social classes. Young interprets
this trend as a 'filtering down' of what, on past evidence, were attitudes held mainly by the more highly educated people in society
(Table 8.1). This analysis is sustained by responses to the 1990 survey
as well. It could equally be explained by the emergence of a new
'service class' as Urry suggests.

161

Table 8.1: Change since 1985 in percentage saying that the countryside has changed
Source: Young, 1989

	Change since 1985 in percentage saying that...	
	...the countryside has changed for the worse	...they are "very concerned' about countryside change
Current residence		
big city	+15	+11
suburbs	0	+12
small city or town	+10	+13
country	+7	+18
Men		
18–34	+18	+14
35–54	-2	+12
55+	+10	+18
Women		
18–34	+9	+6
35–54	+1	+15
55+	+7	+14
Highest qualification		
degree	+1	+5
professional	+5	+19
GCE or CSE	+10	+11
foreign/other/none	+5	+14

Table 8.2: Sources of threat to the countryside
Source: Young, 1989

	Sources of threat to the countryside	
	Greatest threat	Next greatest threat
Urbanisation		
industrial pollution	32	21
urban growth	16	12
motorways and roads	11	11
Agriculture		
chemicals and pesticides	18	26
removal of the landscape	11	12
Recreation		
litter	9	12
tourism and visitors	1	2

Of equal note is the fact that when asked about the sources of threat to the countryside, most respondents regarded threats from industrial pollution and agriculture as more important than threats from tourism and visitors (Table 8.2). At this aggregate level of analysis therefore, there appears to be some suggestion that the custodial role of agriculture, if not farmers, is being challenged by a wide constituency and that recreation and tourism are not the threat many planners and landowners regard them to be. Whether or not such responses can be regarded as wide support for increased access to the countryside is less clear. However, when linked with responses to a question which asked about the 'best options' for land no longer needed for farming, in which recreational and amenity uses scored highly – (64% regarded the creation of National Parks and wildlife reserves as the best or next best options), the survey does suggest that recreational uses of the countryside are regarded as acceptable to the majority of people. In this sense, recreation is not regarded as 'development' and the paradox of tourism, whereby visitors 'destroy' what they came to enjoy, finds little public support (Young, 1989).

In the knowledge that the countryside still serves as a repository for people's ideals and aspirations, it is not surprising to find that the survey reveals general concern about undesirable changes in the countryside. But it also reveals variations in responses linked to place of residence and with people's direct experience of the countryside. So for example, most concern about changes was expressed by those who live in the countryside and by those who had visited the countryside recently. Similarly, regional variations in replies reflected the development pressures experienced in particular parts of the countryside. But although social surveys of this kind provide some indications of how environmental attitudes relate to conventional divisions of class and they provide some insights into how environmental attitudes may be linked to other aspects of social change, they take for granted that the term countryside is itself uncontested.

By contrast, in-depth studies show that the term 'countryside' has different meanings for people; meanings which in part reflect class differences but which also reflect the *nature* of personal experiences. So, although many more people now live in areas close to the countryside and 84% of the public visit the countryside in a year, the nature of that experience has a crucial influence on attitudes towards the countryside. Positive experiences reinforce attachments to the countryside whereas 'bad' experiences provoke unease and unpredictable responses. Whether or not positive experiences predominate is likely to depend on whether the persistence of the countryside aesthetic enables sufficient people to enjoy the kind of countryside they desire. In particular, how the countryside around towns and expanded settlements is to be enjoyed is likely to prove a significant source of friction.

Urban-fringe areas already provoke debate because it is here that the dialectic relationship between the town and the country finds its most potent expression. It is here too where some of the most rapid social change is taking place and where conflicts over access and use are likely to intensify. Because changing social structure favours a de-segregation of cultural values, it is unlikely that a single policy instrument such as the Green Belt or recreational policies such as grant-aid to Country Parks or Countryside Management which depend upon the maintenance of the countryside aesthetic for their 'success', will be capable of providing the kinds of leisure experiences people want or of conserving the kinds of countrysides people desire access to. On the other hand, selective legislation that is designed to extend and widen recreational access to the farmed and settled countryside in these urban-fringe areas might find support amongst the public at large. Linked to strategic and local plans which elevate leisure uses of the countryside to a position on a par with industry and settlement and supported by a strong planning system which integrates outdoor uses of the countryside with transport and environmental policies, the countryside aesthetic could be challenged by new alliances of interests, including local authorities, private landowners and recreational organizations. Recent Countryside Premium and Stewardship Schemes proposed by the Ministry of Agriculture and the Countryside Commission (1989c) make provision for improved access and farm-based leisure activities. But crucial to the argument advanced here is the fact that the kinds of access arrangements and facilities they cater for, are still predicated on the preservation of 'the countryside aesthetic'. They will do little to advance the interests of the growing number of active sports requiring access to the countryside; neither will they enhance the social meaning of the countryside so many hanker after if the schemes are displaced socially, economically and environmentally from the wider countryside of rural and urban-fringe localities.

A rationale for public sector involvement in countryside recreation

The history of public sector involvement in countryside recreation reveals that legislation and public policy has been used to advance the cause of only selective recreational interests and not others (Travis, 1979, Travis et al. 1981). In part this has been a consequence of the areal responsibilities of the Countryside Commission on the one hand with its rural concern and the Sports Council on the other with its essentially urban concern. As a result even recently prepared Regional Recreation Strategies for the countryside ignore provision for countryside sport and others amount to little more than Rights of

Way strategies (Scott, 1990). Notwithstanding the institutionalization of recreation in this way, the essence of what countryside recreation means as revealed through these strategies suggests that 'quiet enjoyment' still remains the guiding principle for both provision and management. Like the values embodied in the National Parks Act, these values seem remarkably out of tune with large sections of the society of the time and scant attention is paid to how people can engage with the better social world the countryside represents or with the opportunity to undertake in an informal way, the wide range of popular outdoor pursuits rising demand indicates.

The union of the Countryside Commissions for Wales and Scotland with the Nature Conservancy Council in these regions may well further distance these agencies from popular values. A reassertion of the supposedly value-free concepts such as carrying capacity linked with the ethos of quiet enjoyment of the countryside, may well result in these hybrid agencies being predispo,ed to defend the countryside aesthetic rather than the enjoyment of the countryside and an active engagement with the better natural and social worlds the countryside represents. While the separate Countryside Commission for England may be better placed to act in the interests of recreationists, without also addressing the place of outdoor sports in the wider countryside, even this latter agency will be poorly placed to serve the full range of recreational interests present in modern society. Identifying a rationale for public sector involvement in countryside recreation thus demands a new vision and one that is informed by social and cultural ideals as well as by empirical study.

In using empirical studies to assess the validity of a number of assumptions which have been used to justify public intervention in countryside recreation in the past, several findings are important:

* At a national level the countryside of the urban fringe is more heavily used than the more distant countryside. Directing public investment to urban fringe areas can therefore be justified on the grounds that these areas appeal to large numbers of the public. Whether or not such involvement should be directed to grant-aid sites managed specifically for recreation such as Country Parks or Regional Parks, or to a concern for extending the range of recreational opportunities in the wider countryside, is more debatable.

* National, regional and sub-regional studies show that much of the recreational use of urban-fringe areas is dispersed rather than concentrated on one or two popular sites or destinations but, the number of visitors recorded at sites managed for recreation, such as Country Parks and other public open-spaces, is highly variable.

165

Explanations for this high variability lie partly in the fact that some sites have a long tradition of use while others are more recent additions to the recreational resource and are less well known. Sites differ too in the range of environments and activities they offer and although there is some evidence to suggest that when Country Parks mount specific events, like Country Fairs or Fun Days, their clientele is drawn from a wider social spectrum than is the case when low-key provision prevails, so few systematic surveys have been completed that it is difficult to explain popularity in these terms alone. Given the evidence from qualitative studies which suggests that peoples' motives for visiting the countryside are often prompted by social factors, events which promote social interaction in pleasant, naturalistic environments are likely to attract people from a wide cross section of society – including those people who only visit the countryside very occasionally. Focusing recreational provision on particular sites then has some merit because a range of social and outdoor activities can be provided in pleasant surroundings – benefits which the private sector has long taken advantage of but which the public sector has largely shunned. Importantly however, any socially beneficial use of such sites is only likely to be achieved if close attention is given to the constituency of users each particular site can attract.

※ The precise location of sites in relation to residential areas as well as the range of facilities and social events offered, appears to exert a profound influence on the kind of use individual sites experience. When sites are located right at the urban edge and are close to residential areas,the local population living within walking distance of the site will contribute the highest proportion of users at that site. In turn, the kinds of uses the site is put to will reflect the interests and activities enjoyed by that local population. The Study of Four Parks around Glasgow demonstrated these relationships very clearly as did the findings of several site surveys undertaken in the South London Green Belt. Thus, the recreational role played by sites in the urban fringe will differ depending upon their ease of access to local people who walk or cycle to them and not necessarily on the recreational preferences of a wider constituency served by car.

※ The range of uses each site is expected to play and the way in which these uses are accommodated within each site will make different demands on resources and on the styles of management adopted. In turn, the recreational role of countryside areas embedded in the urban area or abutting it is likely to be very different from that of more distant countryside sites. In particular, the recreational role of urban fringe areas will often be shaped by the presence or absence of recreational opportunities provided in the urban area itself, as well as by the kinds of recreational uses a local constituency wants. Moulding recreational provision to meet demand is then likely to involve detailed studies of the roles open spaces play in peoples' lives rather than assumptions about a site's putative recreational role based on its position on one side or other of the urban boundary.

※ Present policies presume that Country Parks and urban parks perform differing functions even though detailed studies of how people use these open spaces shows common uses and common appraisals of their environmental and social benefits. Empirical evidence therefore does not support the continued geographical, administrative and functional separation of 'countryside recreation' from other forms of outdoor recreation which take place in urban settings. The absence of any statutory requirement to review the full range of outdoor recreational opportunities available both within the urban area and the surrounding countryside – through structure plans, unitary development plans or local plans, means that this dichotomy will continue. As a result, the spatial disparities in provision revealed by several studies and the differential access to recreational opportunities enjoyed by different user groups detailed by the Access Study and earlier studies, is unlikely to be improved unless local authorities deliberately choose to address them.

※ Critical to removing or easing this disparity in provision and access is the presumption made by providers about the kinds of environments and activities which countryside recreation embraces. For example, it is evident that a number of noisy sports such as motor sports or water sports are not encouraged in Country Parks or on other public open spaces located in the urban fringe. This despite the fact that motor sports for example have a tradition of using urban fringe areas that dates back to the turn of the century (Elson et al. 1986b). For many providers, the appropriate use of the countryside is still regarded as little more than solitary walking so that the peace and quiet of the countryside can be enjoyed and preserved. In modern society, countryside recreation has come to mean much more than peace and quiet and 'having regard to where a site is located' not only involves examining the range of recreational opportunities available in the urban area itself but also discovering what recreational demands an essentially local constituency will make of the countryside (Sports Council, 1990b).

167

※ If one of the overall objectives of public sector intervention in countryside recreation provision is to secure recreational opportunities
which are attractive to a wider cross section of society than currently participates, then these findings suggest that an approach to
planning and managing open-space provision which is genuinely
responsive to the demands of a local constituency is required.
Existing approaches based on open-space standards or upon an
ideology of countryside recreation which endorses particular
behavioural norms and recreational activities because they do not
offend the countryside aesthetic, are not likely to widen participation. The great merit of pursuing a community-sensitive approach
coupled with a locational policy which prioritizes the urban fringe,
is that some urban-fringe neighbourhoods, as for example in
Merseyside and St. Helens and parts of outer London are economically and environmentally disadvantaged. They also house many
people who have no recent tradition of visiting the countryside but
who express a desire to visit the countryside more often. Merely
providing Country Parks in the urban fringe however, will not
prove socially beneficial unless provision is also linked to detailed
studies of people's recreational preferences and environmental
values as well as to studies which can reveal how personal circumstances and experiences impinge on recreational behaviour
(Bacon, 1980). Studies such as Operation Gateway show that the
cost of getting to the countryside is often an excuse rather than the
cause of non-participation amongst some urban residents. They
also show that improving public transport facilities to countryside
destinations without also providing a sustained marketing effort
will not raise participation rates either. Even an 'out-reach'
approach, will not necessarily enhance peoples lives unless what is
provided at the destination proves to be pleasurable. The real
question then becomes 'Can the public sector provide the range of
pleasurable recreational experiences people seek without also
admitting that new provision will challenge the countryside
aesthetic?'

※ In the final analysis countryside recreation is about FUN, not just
peace and quiet. At a time when broader social and cultural
changes suggest that the 'peace and quiet' of the countryside may
not retain the same symbolic significance it has achieved to date in
dominating public debates about the recreational use of the countryside, the public sector is uniquely positioned to develop new
entrepreneurial and innovative approaches which mesh well with
the underlying values of contemporary society. How public authorities choose to become involved will depend crucially upon
whether countryside recreation is to be regarded as a luxury to be

afforded by those with the inclination and ability to pay, or as a basic right that provides all citizens with both metaphorical and real 'gateways to a better physical and social world'. Only when the latter goal achieves a dominant position in society will the centrality of private property rights be challenged and with it the ideology of the countryside aesthetic. In the short term, providers in the public sector need to reassess their own attitudes to what countryside recreation means and to demonstrate a sensitivity and commitment to providing the range of pleasurable experiences all sections of the public expect to find – especially in the farmed and settled countryside.

Bibliography

Abercrombie, P. 1945. *Greater London plan*. 1944. HMSO: London.

Anderson, M. 1981. *Historical perspectives on the role for AONBs: Recreation or Preservation?* Occasional paper 3, Department of Environmental Studies and Countryside Planning. Wye College: University of London.

Applied Leisure Marketing, 1985. *Leisure trips in the countryside*. Applied Leisure Marketing Ltd: London.

Bacon, A.W. 1980. *Land and leisure in an urban landscape*. Centre for Leisure Studies: University of Salford.

Bailey, P. 1978. *Leisure and class in Victorian England*. Routledge: London.

Bannister, C. and Groome, D. (eds) 1984. *Out and about*. Manchester University: Department of Town and Country Planning.

Benington, J. and White, J. (eds) 1988. *The future of leisure services*. Longman: London.

Bennett, T., Mercer, C. and Woollacott, J. 1986. *Popular culture and social relations*. Open University Press: Milton Keynes.

Bernard, M. 1983. Leisure defined: a review of the literature. *Leisure, Recreation and Tourism Abstracts* 8 (1), 1–9.

Blacksell, M. and Gilg, A.W. 1981. *The countryside: planning and change*. George Allen & Unwin: London.

Blunden, J. and Curry, N. 1989. *A people's charter?* Countryside Commission. HMSO: London.

Boaden, N. 1989. 'Evaluating the experience'. In *Breaking new ground*. Ed: M. Bradshaw. pp.14–18. Groundwork Foundation: Birmingham.

Bradley, C. 1986. *Community involvement in greening*. The Groundwork Foundation: Birmingham.

Bradshaw, A.D., Goode, D.A. and Thorp, E. 1986. *Ecology and design in landscape*. Blackwell Scientific Publications: Oxford.

Bromley, P. 1990. *Countryside management*. Spon: London.

Brotherton, I. 1975. 'The development and management of country parks in England and Wales'. *Biol. Conserv.* 7, 171–184.

Burgess, J. 1990. 'The production and consumption of environmental meanings in the mass media: a research agenda for the 1990s'. *Trans. Inst. Br. Geogr.* NS.15, 139–161.

Burgess, J., Limb, M. and Harrison, C.M. 1988a. 'Exploring environmental values through the medium of small groups.' Part One: theory and practice. *Environment and Planning A*, 20, 309–326.

Burgess, J., Limb, M. and Harrison, C.M. 1988b. 'Exploring environmental values through the medium of small groups. Part Two: illustrations of a group at work'. *Environment and Planning A*. 20. 457–476.

Buttel, F.H. and Johnson, D.E. 1977. 'Dimensions of environmental concern: factor structure, correlates and implications for research.' *Environment and Behaviour*. 10, 433–50.

Centre for Leisure Research, 1986. *A digest of sports statistics for the UK.* 2nd ed. Information Series No. 7. Sports Council: London.

Cherry, G.E. 1975. *Environmental planning 1939–1969*. Vol. II. National parks and recreation in the countryside. HMSO: London.

Cherry, G.E. 1985. 'Scenic heritage and national park lobbies and legislation in England and Wales'. *Leisure Studies* 4, 127–139.

Coalter, F. 1985. 'The defence of public leisure services: professional rationality or political struggle?' *Leisure Management*. Vol. 5, No. 5.

Coalter, F. Long, J.A. and Duffield, B.S. 1986. *The rationale for public sector investment in leisure.* Sports Council and Social Science Research Council: London.

Collis, I. 1990. 'Groundwork – fact and fiction'. *Ecos* 11(4) 34–42.

Colne Valley Regional Park Standing Conference 1972. *Colne Valley – strategy for a regional park.* GLC: London.

Commission of the European Communities, 1987. *The Europeans and their environment in 1986.* CEC: Brussels.

Cotgrove, S. and Duff, A. 1981. 'Environmentalism, values and social change'. *British Journal of Sociology*. 32, 92–110.

Council of Nature, 1966. *'The countryside in 1970'.* Proceedings. Council for Nature: London.

Countryside Commission, 1974a. *Advice notes on country parks.* Countryside Commission: Cheltenham.

Countryside Commission, 1974b. *Upland management experiment.* CCP 82. Countryside Commission: Cheltenham.

Countryside Commission, 1976a. *Public transport for countryside recreation.* CCP 94. HMSO: London.

Countryside Commission, 1976b. *The Bollin Valley – a study of land management in the urban fringe*. CCP 97. Countryside Commission: Cheltenham.

Countryside Commission, 1976c. *The Lake District upland management experiment*. CCP 93. Countryside Commission: Cheltenham.

Countryside Commission, 1977a. *Study of informal recreation in South East England (SIRSEE) county site studies*. Volumes 1–4. Summary report and technical report. Countryside Commission: Cheltenham.

Countryside Commission, 1977b. *Study of informal recreation in South East England (SIRSEE)*. Demand report and appendices. Countryside Commission: Cheltenham.

Countryside Commission, 1977c. *Study of informal recreation in South East England (SIRSEE)*. Summary report for the site studies. Countryside Commission working paper. Countryside Commission: Cheltenham.

Countryside Commission, 1978a. *Local authority countryside management projects*. Advisory Series, No. 10 Countryside Commission: Cheltenham.

Countryside Commission, 1978b. *Countryside for all?: A review of the use people make of the countryside for recreation*. CRRAG Conference, York University. Countryside Commission: Cheltenham.

Countryside Commission, 1978c. *A study of management agreements*. CCP 114. Countryside Commission: Cheltenham.

Countryside Commission, 1979. *Ruffold Park marketing study*. CCP 129. Countryside Commission: Cheltenham.

Countryside Commission, 1980a. *Trends in tourism and recreation, 1968–78*. CCP 134. Countryside Commission: Cheltenham.

Countryside Commission, 1980b. *Explore your local countryside*. CCP 135. Countryside Commission: Cheltenham.

Countryside Commission, 1981. *Countryside management in the urban fringe*. CCP 136. Countryside Commission: Cheltenham.

Countryside Commission, 1982a. *Participation in informal recreation: a comparison of two household surveys of informal countryside recreation*. CCP 152. Countryside Commission: Cheltenham.

Countryside Commission, 1982b. *Cannock Chase: the preparation of a country park management plan*. CCP 154. Countryside Commission: Cheltenham.

Countryside Commission, 1982c. *An experiment continued: countryside management in the urban fringe of Barnet and South Hertfordshire*. CCP 148. Countryside Commission: Cheltenham.

Countryside Commission, 1983. *A management plan for the green belt area in Barnet and South Havering*. CCP 147. Countryside Commission: Cheltenham.

Countryside Commission, 1985a. *National countryside recreation survey 1984*. CCP 201. Countryside Commission: Cheltenham.

Countryside Commission, 1985b. *The Wayfarer Project.* CCP 193. Countryside Commission: Cheltenham.

Countryside Commission, 1986a. *Access to the countryside for recreation and sport.* CCP 217 Countryside Commission: Cheltenham.

Countryside Commission, 1986b. *Common land.* The report of the Common Land Forum. CCP215. Countryside Commission: Cheltenham.

Countryside Commission, 1987a. *Enjoying the countryside: priorities for action.* CCP 235. Countryside Commission: Cheltenham.

Countryside Commission, 1987b. *Enjoying the countryside.* A consultation paper on future policies. CCP 225. Countryside Commission: Cheltenham.

Countryside Commission, 1987c. *Policies for enjoying the countryside.* CCP 234. Countryside Commission: Cheltenham.

Countryside Commission, 1987d. *Public transport to the countryside. A marketing handbook for operators and local authorities.* CCP 227. Countryside Commission:Cheltenham.

Countryside Commission, 1987e. *Out in the country. Where you can go and what you can do.* CCP 186. Countryside Commission: Cheltenham.

Countryside Commission, 1988. *Compendium of recreation statistics.* Countryside Commission: Cheltenham.

Countryside Commission, 1989a. *Recreational cycling in the countryside.* CCP 259. Countryside Commission: Cheltenham.

Countryside Commission, 1989b. *A countryside for everyone: an advisory booklet.* CCP 265. Countryside Commission: Cheltenham.

Countryside Commission, 1989c. *Development pressures in the National Parks, 1983–88.* CCD 50. Countryside Commission: Cheltenham.

Countryside Commission, 1989d. *The countryside premium for set-aside land.* CCP 267. Countryside Commission: Cheltenham.

Countryside Commission, 1990. *National rights of way condition survey 1988.* CCP284. Countryside Commission: Cheltenham.

Countryside Commission and Forestry Commission, 1989. *Forests for the community.* CCP 270. Countryside Commission: Cheltenham.

Countryside Commission for Scotland, 1974. *'A park system for Scotland'.* The Commission: Perth.

Countryside Commission for Scotland, 1987. *Countryside around towns in Scotland.* A review of change, 1976–1985. The Commission: Perth.

Countryside Commission and Sports Council, 1984. *Access to the countryside for recreation and sport: issues for consultation.* CCP 166. Countryside Commission: Cheltenham.

Countryside Review Committee, 1977. *Leisure in the countryside.* Topic Paper 2. HMSO: London.

Cox, G. 1988 '"Reading" nature: reflections on ideological persistence and the politics of the countryside'. *Landscape Research*, 13 (3), 24–34.

Cracknell, B. 1967. 'Accessibility to the countryside as a factor in planning for leisure'. *Regional Studies* 1, 21–57, 157.

Cunningham, H. 1980. *Leisure in the industrial revolution.* Croom Helm: London.

Curry, N. 1985. 'Countryside recreation sites policy – a review'. *Town Planning Review.* 56, 70–89.

Curry, N. and Comley, A. 1986. Who enjoys the countryside? Strathclyde Papers in Planning. University of Strathclyde: Glasgow.

Davidson, J. and Wibberley, G.P. 1977. *Planning and the rural environment.* Pergamon Press: Oxford.

Department of the Environment (DOE), 1975a. *Recreation and deprivation in inner urban areas.* HMSO: London.

Department of the Environment, 1975b. *'Sport and Recreation'.* White Paper (Cmnd. 6200). HMSO: London.

Department of the Environment, 1976. *Regional councils for sport and recreation.* Circular 47/76. Department of the Environment: London.

Donnelly, P. 1986. 'The paradox of parks: politics of recreational land use before and after mass trespasses.' *Leisure Studies* 5 (2), 211–231.

Dorset County Council, 1986. *South-East Dorset urban fringe project.* Consultative Document. Dorset County Council: Dorchester.

Dower, J. 1945. *National Parks in England and Wales.* Cmnd. 6628. HMSO: London.

Dower, M. 1965. *Fourth wave: the challenge of leisure.* Civic Trust: London.

Dower, M., Rapoport, R., Strelitz, Z., Kew, S. 1981. *Leisure provision and people's needs.* HMSO: London.

Duffield, B.S. 1985. 'A review of mobility and countryside recreation'. In: *Countryside recreation in the 1980s: current research and future challenges.* pp. 112–128. Countryside Recreation Research Group: Cheltenham.

Duffield, B.S. and Owen, M.L. 1971. *Leisure and countryside. A geographical appraisal of countryside recreation in the Edinburgh area.* University of Edinburgh: Edinburgh.

Elson, M.J. 1977. *A review and evaluation of recreation site surveys.*
Working Paper 9. Countryside Commission: Cheltenham.

Elson, M.J. 1979a. *Countryside trip making.* State of the art review No. 12.
Sports Council – Social Science Research Council. Joint Panel on Sport
and Leisure Research: London.

Elson, M.J. 1979b. *The urban fringe: open land policies and programmes in
the metropolitan counties.* Working Paper WP14.
Countryside Commission: Cheltenham.

Elson, M.J. 1979c. *The leisure use of green belts and urban fringes.*
Sports Council and Social Science Research Council: London.

Elson, M.J. 1986. *Green belts: conflict mediation in the urban fringe.*
Heinemann: London.

Elson, M.J., Buller, H. and Stanley, P. 1986a. *Getting into gear: land-based
motorsports in the 1980s.* The Sports Council: London.

Elson, M.J., Buller, H. and Stanley, P.A. 1986b. *Motorsports: from image to
reality.* Sports Council Research Report No. 30. Sports Council: London.

Elson, M.J. and Sienkiewicz. 1977. *Study of informal recreation in South East
England – the site studies.* Summary Report. Countryside Commission:
Cheltenham.

English Tourist Board, 1983. *Leisure day trips in Great Britain: Summer 1981
and 1982.* English Tourist Board: London.

English Tourist Board, 1988. *Visitors in the countryside.*
English Tourist Board: London.

Ferguson, M.J. and Munton, R.J.C. 1978. Informal recreation in the urban
fringe: Provision and management of sites in London's Green Belt.
Working Paper No.2. Land for informal recreation.
Department of Geography: University College London.

Ferguson, M.J. and Munton, R.J.C. 1979. 'Informal recreation sites in
London's green belt'. *Area* 11, 196–205.

Fitton, M. 1976. 'The urban fringe and the less privileged'.
Countryside Recreation Review 1, 25–34.

Fitton, M. 1978. 'The reality – for whom are we actually providing?'
In: *Countryside for all?: a review of the use people make of the
countryside for recreation.* pp. 38–67. CRRAG Conference, York
University. Countryside Commission: Cheltenham.

Fitton, M. 1979. 'Countryside recreation – the problems of opportunity'.
Local Government Studies 5, 57–90.

Gibbs, R.S. and Whitby, M.C. 1975. *Local authority expenditure on access
land.* Agriculture Adjustment Unit: University of Newcastle-upon-Tyne.

Glyptis, S. 1991. *Countryside recreation.* Longman: London.

Greater London Council, 1975–6. *Greater London recreation study.*
Research report 19, parts 1–3. Greater London Council: London.

Greater London and South East Council for Sport and Recreation, (GLSECSR)
1979. *Issues report.* Regional recreation strategy subject report. Greater
London and South East Council for Sport and Recreation. London.

Greater London and South East Council for Sport and Recreation, 1981.
Towards greater participation in sport and recreation. Regional
recreation strategy subject report. Greater London and South East
Council for Sport and Recreation: London.

Greater London and South East Council for Sport and Recreation, 1982.
Prospect for the eighties. Regional recreation strategy. Greater London
and South East Council for Sport and Recreation: London.

Greater London and South East Council for Sport and Recreation, 1984.
Recreation in the metropolitan green belt. Greater London and South
East Council for Sport and Recreation: London.

Green, B. 1981. *Countryside conservation.* George Allen and Unwin: London.

Green, E., Hebron, S. and Woodward, D. 1987. *Leisure and gender.*
The Sports Council and Economic and Social Research Council: London.

Greening, P.A.K. and Slater, P. 1984. *Rural recreational transport: the Sunday
bus experiment.* T.R.R.L. laboratory report, 1026. Transport and Road
Research Laboratory: Stevenage.

Groome, D. and Tarrant, C. 1984. 'Countryside recreation: achieving access
for all?'. *Countryside Planning Year Book 1984*; 77–98.

Groundwork Foundation, 1986. *Putting wasteland to good use.*
Groundwork Foundation: Birmingham.

HMSO, 1988. *Social Trends.* HMSO:London

Hall, A. 1976. Management in the urban fringe.
Countryside Recreation Review 1, 8–13.

Hall, P., Gracey, H., Drewett, R. and Thomas, R. 1973.
The containment of urban England. George Allen and Unwin: London.

Hampshire County Council, 1971. *Conservation of the New Forest.*
Hampshire County Council: Winchester.

Hampshire County Council, 1987. *Countryside recreation policies.*
Hampshire County Council: Winchester.

Hardy, D. and Ward, C. 1981. *The plotlands of the Thames valley.* Geography
and Planning Papers, No.4. Middlesex Polytechnic: London.

Harrison, C.M. 1981. Preliminary results of a survey of site use in the South
London Green Belt. *Working Paper No.9. Land for informal recreation.*
Department of Geography: University College London.

Harrison, C.M. 1983. 'Countryside recreation and London's urban fringe'. *Trans. Inst. Br. Geogr.* 8, 295–313.

Harrison, C.M., Limb, M. and Burgess, J. 1986a. 'Recreation 2000: views of the country from the city'. *Landscape Research*, 11, 19–24.

Harrison, C.M., Limb, M. and Burgess, J. 1986b. *Popular values for the countryside.* A report to the Countryside Commission. University College London: London.

Home, R. 1987. *Planning use classes.* BSP Professional Books: Oxford.

Howard, E. 1898. *Garden cities of tomorrow.* Faber: London.

Inglehart, R. 1977. *The silent revolution: changing values and political styles among Western Publics.* Princeton University Press: Princeton.

Joad, C.E.M. 1935. *Diogenes or the future of leisure.* Kegan Paul, Trensch Trubner: London.

Lash, S. and Urry, J. 1987. *The end of organized capitalism.* Polity: Cambridge.

Land Use Consultants Limited, 1984. *London's green belt: a handbook for action.* Greater London and South East Council for Sport and Recreation: London.

Lavery, P. 1983. 'Countryside management schemes in the urban fringe'. *Planning Outlook*, 25: 52–9.

Laurie, I.C. (ed). 1974. *Nature in cities.* Wiley: Chichester.

Law, S. and Perry, N. 1971. Countryside recreation for Londoners – a preliminary research approach. *Greater London Council Intelligence Unit Quarterly Bulletin*, No. 14. 11–26.

Layton, R. 1985. 'Recreation, management and landscape in Epping Forest: c. 1800–1984'. *Field Studies* (6) 269–290.

Lee Valley Regional Park Authority, 1987. *2 million reasons why Lee Valley Park is a success story.* Lee Valley Regional Park Authority Annual Report 1986–87.

Le Motte, S. 1984. *Operation gateway.* Report no. 1 and 2. Pilot and implementation stage. Nottingham County Council: Nottingham.

Limb, M. 1986a. 'Community involvement in leisure provision – private enterprise or public interest?' In: *'Leisure: politics, planning and people'*, pp. 90–110. Vol. 3. The politics of leisure ed. F. Coalter. Leisure Studies Association: London.

Limb, M. 1986b. *Community involvement in the management of open space for recreation in the urban fringe.* PhD. University of London: London.

London County Council, 1950. *Administrative county of London development plan.* The Council: London.

London County Council, 1964. *Parks for tomorrow.* The Council: London.

Lowe, P. and Goyder, J. 1983. *Environmental groups in politics.* George Allen and Unwin: London.

Lowe, P. and Flynn, A. 1989. 'Environmental planning under the Thatcher government'. *Ecos.* 10 (4). 22–29.

Mabey, R. 1980. *The common ground.* Hutchinson: London.

MAS Survey Research Limited. 1984. *Survey of knowledge and interest about the countryside.* Report to the Countryside Commission: Cheltenham.

Market Opinion Research International Limited, 1987. *Public attitudes towards nature conservation.* Research study conducted for Nature Conservancy Council. MORI: London.

Maslow, A. 1969. *Toward a psychology of being.* Harper Row: New York.

MacEwen, A. and MacEwen, M. 1982. *National parks: conservation or cosmetics?* George Allen and Unwin: London.

McIntosh, P. and Charlton, V. 1985. *The impact of sport for all policy.* Sports Council: London.

Mays, N. (ed) 1982. *Countryside recreation in the 1980s: current research and future challenges.* Proceedings of Countryside Recreation Research Group Conference. CRRAG: Bristol.

Miller, F.A. and Tranter, R.B. (eds) 1988. *Public perception of the countryside.* Centre for Agricultural Strategy: Reading.

Mercer, D. 1973. The concept of recreational need. *J. Leisure Research* 5, 37–50.

Mercer, D. 1979. 'Outdoor recreation: contemporary research and policy issues'. *Progress in resource management and planning.* Vol. 1. 87–142. Eds. T. O'Riordan and R.C. D'Argi. Wiley: Chichester.

Ministry of Housing and Local Government, 1955. *Green belts.* Circular 42/55. HMSO: London.

Ministry of Housing and Local Government, 1957. *Green belts.* Circular 50/57. HMSO: London.

Ministry of Land and Natural Resources, 1966. *Leisure in the countryside.* HMSO: London.

Moore, N.W. 1987. *The bird of time.* Cambridge University Press: Cambridge.

Mostyn, B.J. 1979. *Personal benefits and satisfactions derived from participating in urban wildlife projects: a qualitative evaluation.* Nature Conservancy Council: Peterborough.

Munton, R.J.C. 1983. *London's green belt: containment in practice.* George Allen and Unwin: London.

Nash, R.N. 1967. *Wilderness and the American mind.* Yale University: Yale.

Newby, H. 1979. *Green and pleasant land? Social change in rural England.* Hutchinson: London.

Newby, H. 1988. *The countryside in question.* Hutchinson: London.

Office of Population Censuses and Surveys (OPCS), 1976. *General household survey, 1973.* HMSO: London.

Office of Population Censuses and Surveys, 1979. *General household survey, 1977.* HMSO: London.

Office of Population Censuses and Surveys, 1989. *General household survey, 1987.* HMSO: London.

O'Riordan, T. 1976. *Environmentalism.* Pion: London.

Patmore, J.A. 1978. *Recreation and Resources.* Blackwells: Cambridge.

Patmore, J.A. and Rodgers, H.B. (eds) 1973. *Leisure in the north west.* North West Sports Council: Salford.

Penning-Rowsell, E.C. and Lowenthal, D. 1986. *Landscape meanings and values.* George Allen and Unwin: London.

Pepper, D. 1984. *The roots of modern environmentalism.* Croom Helm: London.

Philips, A. and Ashcroft, P. 1987. 'The impact of research in countryside recreation policy development'. *Leisure Studies*, 6, 315–328.

Probert, G. and Hamersley, C. 1978. Gwent's gains from countryside management. *The Surveyor,* 10 Aug, 1978, 14–17.

Qualitative Consultancy, 1986. *Qualitative research to explore motivations behind visiting the countryside – final report.* Report to Countryside Commission: Cheltenham.

Rapoport, R. and Rapoport, R.N. 1975. *Leisure and the family life cycle.* Routledge and Kegan Paul: London.

Roberts, K. 1978. *Countryside recreation and social class.* Unpublished report to the Countryside Commission: Cheltenham.

Roberts, K. and Thompson, C.J. 1981. Recreation visiting patterns among users of some informal recreation sites in London's Green Belt. *Working Paper No.11 'Land for informal recreation'.* Department of Geography: University College London.

Scott, P. 1990. 'Recreation 2000 – setting the agenda for countryside recreation'. *Ecos.* 11(2), 40–43.

Select Committee of the House of Lords on Sport and Leisure, 1973. *Second Report.* HMSO: London.

Sharp. E. 1984. The implementation of land-use policy in the urban fringe: the North Middlesex Green Belt estates. In: *The Changing Countryside.* pp.261–275. Eds: Clark, G., Groenendijk, J. and Thissem, F. Geobooks: Norwich.

179

Sheail, J. 1976. *Nature in trust: the history of nature conservation in Britain.* Blackie: Glasgow

Sheail, J. 1981. *Rural conservation in inter-war Britain.* Clarendon Press: Oxford.

Sheail, J. 1985. *Pesticides and nature conservation. The British experience 1950–75.* Clarendon Press: Oxford.

Sheail, J. 1988. 'The great divide: an historical perspective'. *Landscape Research* 13 (1), 2–5.

Shoard, M. 1987. *This land is our land.* Paladin: London.

Sidaway, R. 1985. 'Trends and issues in countryside recreation in the 1970s and 1980s: analysis and interpretation of recent large-scale participation surveys'. In: *Countryside Recreation in the 1980s: current research and future challenges,* pp 2–29. CRRAG: Bristol.

Sidaway, R. 1988. *Sport, recreation and nature conservation.* Sports Council: London

Sidaway, R. 1990. *Birds and walkers.* Ramblers' Association: London.

Sidaway, R. 1991. *Good conservation practice for sport and recreation.* Sports Council: London.

Sidaway, R. and Duffield, B.S. 1984. 'A new look at countryside recreation in the urban fringe'. *Leisure Studies,* 3, 249–271.

Slee, W. 1982. *An evaluation of country park policy.* Gloucestershire papers in local and rural planning, No. 16. GLOSCAT: Cheltenham.

Sports Council, 1982. *Sport in the community – the next ten years.* Sports Council: London.

Sports Council, 1983. *Leisure policy for the future.* Sports Council: London.

Sports Council, 1990. *A countryside for sport.* Sports Council: London.

Sports Council and Countryside Commission, 1990. *Motorized sports in the countryside: overcoming the challenges.* Sports Council: London.

Sports Council and Economic and Social Research Council, 1986. *Work and leisure in the 1980s.* ed. N. Lloyd. Sports Council and Economic and Social Research Council: London.

Standing Conference on London and South East Regional Planning, (SCLSERP) 1976. *The improvement of London's green belt.* SC620: London.

Standing Conference on London and South East Regional Planning, 1979. *Policies towards provision of recreation facilities in London's green belt.* Report by the Green Belt Working Group. SC1111 Revised: London.

Standing Conference on London and South East Regional Planning. 1981. *South East Regional planning: the 1980s.* SC1500: London.

Stockdale, J. 1985. *What is leisure? An empirical analysis of the concept of leisure and the role of leisure in people's lives.* Sports Council and Economic and Social Research Council: London.

Suffolk County Council. 1976. *Suffolk heritage coast: draft plan.* Suffolk County Council: Bury.

Thomas, K. 1984. *Man and the natural world: changing attitudes in England 1500–1800.* Penguin: London.

Thomson, K.J. and Whitby, M.C. 1976. The economics of public access to the countryside. *J. Agric. Econ.* 27, 307–320.

Thrift, N. and Williams, P. (eds) 1987. *Class and space: the making of urban society.* Routledge and Kegan Paul: London.

Tourism and Recreation Research Unit Edinburgh, 1983. *Urban parks and open spaces – a review.* Sports Council and Social Science Research Council: London.

Tourism and Recreation Research Unit, 1980. *A study of four parks in and around Glasgow.* Research Report No. 44: Edinburgh.

Travis, A.S. and Veal, A.J. 1976. *Recreation and the urban fringe.* Report of CRRAG Conference, 1975. Centre for Urban and Regional Studies, University of Birmingham: Birmingham.

Travis, A.S. 1979. *The state and leisure provision.* Sports Council and Social Science Research Council: London.

Travis, A.S., Veal, A.J., Duesbury, K. and White, J. 1981. *The role of central government in relation to the provision of leisure services in England and Wales.* Centre for Regional, Urban and Local Government Studies. University of Birmingham Research Monograph 86: Birmingham.

Urry, J. 1988. 'Cultural change and contemporary holiday–making'. *Theory, Culture and Society*, 5, 35–55.

Van Liere, K.D. and Dunlap, R.E. 1980. 'The social bases of environmental concern'. *Public Opinion Quarterly*, 44, 181–197.

Veal, A.J. 1979. *Countryside recreation in England and Wales.* Working Paper 66. Centre for Urban and Regional Studies: Birmingham.

Veal, A.J. 1980. *Trends in leisure participation and problems of forecasting: the state of the art.* Sports Council and Social Science Research Council: London.

Veal, A.J. 1987. *Leisure and the future.* Leisure and Recreation Studies 4. George Allen and Unwin: London.

Veal, A.J. 1989. Leisure, lifestyle and status: a pluralist framework for analysis. *Leisure Studies.* 8 (2), 141–154.

Ward, M. and Hardy, D. 1986. *Goodnight campers: the history of the British holiday camp.* Mansell: London.

White, J. and Dunn, M.C. 1975. *Countryside recreation planning: problems and prospects in the West Midlands.* Occasional Paper No. 33. Centre for Urban and Regional Studies: Birmingham.

Williams, R. 1975. *The country and the city.* Paladin: St Albans.

Wilson, J. 1988. *Politics and Leisure.* Leisure and Recreation Studies 5. Unwin Hyman: London.

Worster, D. 1985. *Nature's economy.* Cambridge University Press: Cambridge.

Young, K. 1989. Rural Prospects. In: *British social attitudes.* The 5th Report. pp.155–174. Eds: Jowell, R., Witherspoon, S. and Brook, L. Gower: Aldershot.

Young, K. 1990. Living under threat. In: *British Social Attitudes.* The 7th Report. pp.77–102. Eds: Jowell, R., Witherspoon, S. and Brook, L. Gower: Aldershot.

Zetter, J.A. 1971. *The evolution of country park policy.* Countryside Commission: Cheltenham.

Index

· ·

CONTINUED

183